Dog Detectives

How to Train Your Dog to Find Lost Pets

Kat Albrecht

Publishing

Wenatchee, Washington U.S.A.

Dog Detectives
How to Train Your Dog to Find Lost Pets
Kat Albrecht

Dogwise Publishing
A Division of Direct Book Service, Inc.
701B Poplar Wenatchee, Washington 98807
1-509-663-9115, 1-800-776-2665
www.dogwisepublishing.com / info@dogwisepublishing.com
© 2008 Kathy Ellen Albrecht

Graphic Design: Nathan Woodward
Indexing: Cheryl Smith
Cover Photo: Cat detection dog Susie plays with Target Cat Cheeto, photograph provided by Jan Jarvis.

Others who contributed photographs for this book were: Schmuel Thaler, Santa Cruz Sentinel; Jill Buchanan; Hardin Weaver; Cannon Hill; Jane Sokolow; Susan Tiftick; Melinda Hearne; Dani Deibert; Don Harris, UCSC Photography Services; Daisy Villicana; and Vicki Vaughn.

Illustrations provided by Sue Gibson.

Library of Congress Cataloging-in-Publication Data

Albrecht, Kat.
  Dog detectives : how to train your dog to find lost pets / Kat Albrecht.
    p. cm.
  ISBN-13: 978-1-929242-48-1
  1. Search dogs--Training. I. Title.
  SF428.73.A43 2008
  636.7'0886--dc22
                                    2007034504
  ISBN: 978-1-929242-48-1
  Printed in the U.S.A.

TABLE OF CONTENTS

DEDICATION

This book is dedicated to Judy Schreiber—private investigator, friend, and MAR Technician graduate who planned to train her Coonhound Billy Jo to trail lost pets. One summer day over lunch in Orlando, Judy encouraged me to continue to believe in my dream of training and certifying pet detectives and search dogs on a national level. Sadly, Judy's dream to become a pet detective was shattered three months later when a car crash left her disabled. I honor Judy with this book and with my continued struggle to believe in my dream.

INTRODUCTION

Life is full of surprises. I know this first hand because one day my dog was secure in my yard and the next thing I knew, he was lost in the woods. One day I was a respected police officer and the next thing I knew, I was a full fledged pet detective.

My background has always been in law enforcement, initially as a 9-1-1 dispatcher, then as a full-time police officer, and later as a detective. My first exposure to working with search dogs was as a police Bloodhound handler. I trained and worked for several years with search dogs to locate physical evidence, criminals and missing persons. My passion became hunting dangerous criminals with Bloodhounds and I absolutely loved my job. My dogs were quite successful in this endeavor: my Bloodhound, A.J., earned the 1995 National Police Bloodhound Association Lifesaving Award for tracking down and saving the life of a man who was shot in the head and would have died in the woods if we hadn't found him in time.

But one spring morning in 1996 my life changed. I went outside to discover A.J. had dug his way out of my yard and was missing. A.J. was not only a highly trained, valuable law enforcement resource and my police partner, he was also my "buddy" and my source of unconditional love. Needless to say, when I saw that he was missing, I panicked.

I didn't do what most other pet owners do when they have lost a pet. I didn't drive to my local shelter. I didn't head over to Kinkos to create lost dog posters. Instead, I did what I was trained to do. Because I was a member of the local search-and-rescue team, I knew that the best chance that I had of finding A.J. was to bring in another trained search-and-rescue dog to track A.J.'s scent.

I immediately called a friend to see if she could bring out her Golden Retriever, Kea. Kea and A.J. had searched together many times for missing people, so I knew she was a talented tracker. I knew that if any dog could find A.J., it was Kea. We had Kea scent A.J.'s bedding and within 20 minutes, Kea tracked A.J. and found him. A.J. was in the neighborhood, sniffing around on a neighbor's front porch. I was so relieved! It took a Golden Retriever to rescue the missing Bloodhound!

Author and her Bloodhound A.J.

In traditional search-and-rescue for missing people, trailing dogs like A.J. and Kea are used to pick up a scent trail and establish a direction of travel and hopefully track right up to the lost person. Before Kea arrived, I spent 20 minutes checking three different directions, uncertain as to which way A.J. had headed. Without Kea, I would have had no idea which direction to start searching for my lost dog.

This incident—losing A.J. and finding him again by using Kea—is what prompted me to ask the question: I know how to train dogs to find lost people—why doesn't someone train dogs to find lost pets? I first posed this question on a search-and-rescue dog discussion list on the Internet back in 1997. At the time, I was still a full-time police officer working a graveyard shift. I had my hands full just working A.J. while training my new Bloodhound puppy, Chase. I had no intention of doing pet detective work. I thought that it was a great project—for someone else to take on.

My recommendation on the Internet was met with a lukewarm response. The general consensus was that it would be a "waste of time" to train a dog to find lost pets because of the amount of time and effort the training would require. Although I didn't appreciate my idea being shot down, I suspected that it just lacked the appeal of traditional search-and-rescue dog training. After all, searching for missing people and working major disasters was noble and likely viewed as a more important task than searching for missing pets.

I tried to put the pet detective idea behind me, but it haunted me. Finally, after six months of not being able to shake the idea, I decided that, as an experiment, I would see if I could train a dog to find lost pets.

In addition to my Bloodhounds, I also had Rachel, an 8-year-old Weimaraner. Rachel was my retired cadaver search dog who I had used on several homicide and evidence cases. Rachel was a great pet detective candidate because she was already trained for scent discrimination work. Whatever scent I placed under her nose, Rachel knew I wanted her to search for that particular scent. If I scented her on a gun, Rachel would search for a gun. If I scented her on toothpaste, Rachel would search for toothpaste. I spent the next four months teaching Rachel to find stationary cats and trail the scent of dogs.

Author and Rachel.

In her first four searches, Rachel found two missing cats and one missing dog. Over the next three years, I used Rachel and my Bloodhounds, A.J. and Chase, on a total of 99 missing-pet investigations with a 69 percent success rate. We searched for lost cats, dogs, snakes, turtles, ferrets, iguanas, and even a gecko who escaped his aquarium. My search dogs and I found pets alive, we found pets deceased, and in some cases we didn't find the pet at all. The response from the pet owners who were lucky enough to have access to our services was always the same: this was a service they valued and that needed to be developed. Their support encouraged me to continue and thus, I began my efforts to train others to work as pet detectives and to form an organization—Missing Pet Partnership—to help professionalize this valuable service.

How This Book Is Organized

This book is organized in such a way to help prepare anyone who wants to become a professional Missing Animal Response technician (or "pet detective"), a person who uses highly trained dogs certified to participate in lost pet searches. I recognize that not everyone who reads this book will want to become a professional or have their dogs certified, and indeed you will see there is a need for volunteers. Regardless of your personal goals, if you master the techniques laid out in this book you will be an asset to your community, be better able to find your own missing pets, or at the very least, gain expertise in the fields of scent discrimination, scent trails, and working with dogs in an endlessly fascinating endeavor.

The book is divided into three major parts. The first four chapters contain an overview of Missing Animal Response work, including the three major search disciplines. Chapters 5 through 7 cover material on scent, lost pet behaviors, and the science of searching. This material may be familiar to readers with a lot of experience in tracking or search-and-rescue. Chapters 8 through 14 cover detailed training plans, opportunities to work in this field on a professional basis, and case studies. The Resources section contains further reading and equipment recommendation and certification tests.

Chapter 1

MISSING PET PARTNERSHIP

Back in 1997 when I initially dabbled in pet detective work, there were already a few pet detectives who offered services, such as distributing lost-pet flyers and searching local animal shelters. While these services were helpful, they failed to offer an aspect that I believe was overlooked: aggressive physical searches for lost pets using investigative law enforcement techniques. Many lost pets, particularly cats, are injured and hiding or trapped and hidden close to home. In cases such as these, posting lost-cat flyers is not the most effective recovery technique. As I moved forward in pet detective work, a key question arose: Who would oversee the national development of lost pet services?

After several years of mistakes, and setbacks, I developed a system for conducting lost pet investigations. While my search dogs were capable of achieving amazing results, I realized they were not the entire answer to finding a lost pet—they were simply one tool within that system. There is a science to finding lost people. Search managers don't simply deploy searchers to wander aimlessly in the woods. They implement an organized plan using highly trained resources, the application of proper techniques and technologies, and proper investigative techniques. I wanted a similar science developed for finding lost pets.

Missing Pet Partnership (MPP), a national nonprofit organization, was born out of my desire to standardize training techniques and offer certification for both the people and dogs who work together to find lost pets. Today, that is the principal mission of MPP (www.missingpetpartnership.com). MPP offers on-line training, seminars, and practical in-field search training to people who want to become certified Missing Animal Response technicians (MAR technicians). MPP also operates Pet Hunters International, the first-ever pet detective academy that trains and certifies MAR technicians (volunteer and for-profit pet detectives), and search dogs to locate lost pets.

In addition to a training program, Missing Pet Partnership provides educational materials to pet owners, veterinarians, and animal shelter and welfare organization workers. MPP plans to conduct further scientific research in the behavioral patterns of lost pets, enabling it to better predict the distances that animals travel when lost.

MAR Technician Training

The lost pet recovery techniques and technologies that I used beginning in 1997 have since been adapted into Missing Pet Partnership's MAR Technician Certification Program. A MAR technician learns how to train cat detection dogs; how to train trailing dogs to track lost dogs; analytical methods such as search probability theory and deductive reasoning to predict the distances that lost pets travel; and the collection and analysis of physical evidence. Technicians also learn how to use high-tech equipment such as amplified listening devices, night vision, and baby monitors. While more detail on training and the certification process is provided later in the book (see Chapters 8 through 11 and the Resource section), following is an overview of what a MAR technician is expected to learn:

- How to evaluate and train dogs for MAR work
- How to identify, collect, and analyze MAR physical evidence
- How to detect deception when interviewing people
- Search strategies
- Deductive reasoning
- Surveillance work
- Search probability theory

- How human and animal behaviors influence recovery efforts
- How and where to search for various species
- How to approach stray dogs
- Proper use of animal capture and detection equipment
- Shelter and neighborhood checks
- Field hazards for the MAR Technician
- Trap-and-reunite (TAR) services
- Loose Dog Recovery (LDR) team training
- Grief counseling for pet owners

Looking to the Future

Through future partnerships with shelters and veterinarians, Missing Pet Partnership hopes to establish a system of pairing former shelter dogs/ MAR dog candidates with MAR technician graduates who want to train a dog to locate lost pets. One of our long-term goals includes building a national training center (near Seattle, WA) to evaluate, house, train, and ultimately distribute certified MAR dogs to entities (individuals, veterinary clinics, shelters, and animal welfare organizations) that plan to offer community-based MAR services. While some MAR technicians may elect to train their own dog in MAR work, there is a clear need to develop a credible national source that provides trained MAR dogs, just as other national service dog organizations train and distribute trained service dogs.

Training a "dog detective" is a serious undertaking. Ask anyone who has ever trained a bomb-detection, drug-detection, cadaver-detection, or a search-and-rescue dog—it is expensive, time consuming, and difficult work. If you remain patient and willing to learn, though, you and your dog can experience the satisfaction of helping to reunite a missing pet with a grieving family. I wish you good luck as you and your dog work toward making a difference in the lives of people and their companion animals.

Chapter 2
MAR Disciplines

Missing Pet Partnership recognizes three different Missing Animal Response dog disciplines:

- Cat-detection
- Trailing
- Dual-purpose

Although there are three different disciplines, there are actually two types of search techniques that are used for searching for lost pets:

- Area searches
- Trailing searches

Cat-detection dogs conduct area searches. Trailing dogs utilize trailing techniques. And dual-purpose dogs are trained to do both area and trailing searches.

Area Searches

Area search means that a dog is used to search a particular area (e.g., the neighborhood in which a cat disappeared) under the direction of a dog handler who attempts to read when the dog first detects the scent of what he is searching for. The handler decides where she will have her dog search, using a systematic search pattern and the cue, "Check this," as she points and asks her dog to sniff all potential hiding places. This is the same method that drug, bomb, and arson dog handlers use when working their detection dogs. An area search can include searching places as varied as woods, residential neighborhoods, farms, orchards, and commercial business districts.

MAR dogs used in area searches are directed to search in garages, backyards, sheds, underneath houses and decks, open fields, and in areas of heavy vegetation. Area search work is not as rigorous as trailing because the handler can walk and stop without affecting the dog.

Area search dogs are used to search every conceivable hiding place within a lost cat's territory.

Cat-detection dog Rachel finishes searching under a deck for a lost cat.

Both cat-detection and dual-purpose dogs are used in area search work. Cat-detection dogs are *always* used to conduct area searches for lost cats while dual-purpose dogs are *sometimes* used to conduct an area search for lost cats or other small pets who are not likely to travel far. When dual-purpose dogs are not conducting area searches, they are used to track the scent trail of a lost dog or other animal by a method called trailing.

Trailing

Trailing means that a dog is used to follow a scent trail while the handler walks or jogs behind, trusting her dog and attempting to read when he has lost the scent. The handler uses little or no strategy because she is virtually at the mercy of where the dog drags her. The typical assignment on almost every such search is to take the MAR trailing dog to the *point last seen* (PLS), present a *scent article* (something with the lost dog's scent) to the dog, and follow behind as you study the trailing dog's body language. The primary job as a MAR trailing dog handler is to study and interpret (or "read") whether or not the dog has the scent, has lost the scent, or is distracted by another scent. Trailing work is rigorous and involves following behind a dog in all types of terrain.

MAR trailing dog Chase follows a scent trail while the handler jogs behind her.

The two types of MAR dogs used in scent discrimination trailing are trailing dogs and, in some cases, dual-purpose dogs. MAR trailing dogs are always used to trail lost dogs, cats, horses, and other animals who are most likely to travel a significant distance. MAR dual-purpose dogs are *sometimes* used to follow the scent trail of a missing animal and other times they are used to conduct area searches to detect the scent of lost pets.

A major difference between reading an area search dog and reading a trailing dog is how he reacts to the presence or the absence of scent. When working an area search dog, you are generally starting in an area that may or may not contain large concentrations of the missing pet's scent. You are usually working the dog in no or low-scent conditions and watching for the dog to *alert* to the sudden presence of airborne scent (*see Diagram 1 page 16*). An alert is a sudden change in body language such as rapid sniffing, tail wiggling, or an obvious change of direction in which the dog shows an obvious determination to find something. When working a trailing dog, though, you are always starting in the presence of the missing pet's scent at the PLS. You are then jogging behind the dog and watching for indications that she has run out of scent (*see Diagram 2 page 17*). When this happens, it can mean that she missed a turn or that the missing pet was removed, possibly placed in a vehicle and transported out of the area. Thus, detection work is somewhat the opposite of trailing since detection dogs (presumably working where there is *no* scent) will indicate at the first hint of a scent, while trailing dogs (presumably working in the scent) will indicate when the scent is no longer there.

Cat-Detection Dogs
MAR cat-detection dogs are specialists in locating lost cats. These dogs are used to search an area for any cat he can find. Just like other detection dogs (bird dogs, drug-detection dogs, bomb-detection dogs), cat-detection dogs are given a simple cue and will search and react when they detect the slightest scent of any cat. If during the course of the search they find the wrong cat, they are simply told, "Good dog—find another!" and they immediately begin to search for more cats.

Training Overview
Cat-detection dogs are trained to locate and pinpoint the source of cat scent. To teach this, a cat is crated and hidden, and the dog is taught to search for him and to alert his handler when he finds the kitty. The exuberant body language normally associated with an alert is what tells the

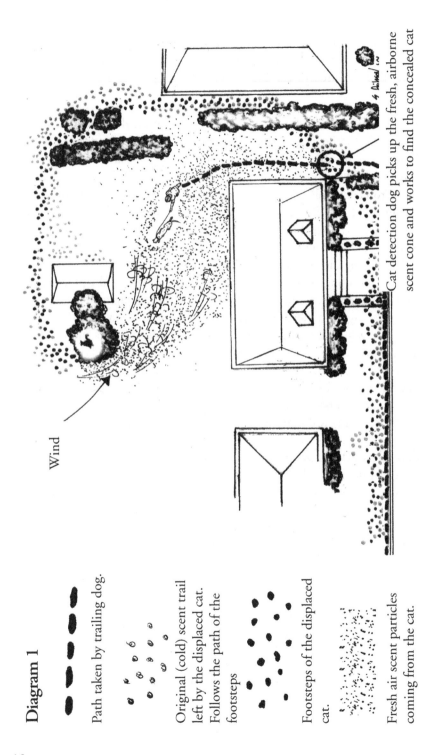

Cat detection dog picks up the fresh, airborne scent cone and works to find the concealed cat

Wind

Diagram 1

Path taken by trailing dog.

Original (cold) scent trail left by the displaced cat. Follows the path of the footsteps

Footsteps of the displaced cat.

Fresh air scent particles coming from the cat.

Diagram 2

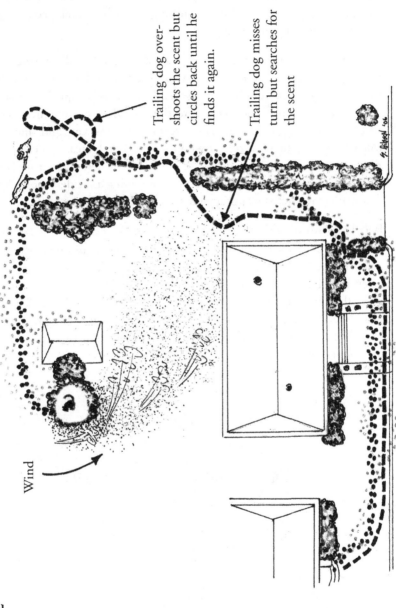

Trailing dog over-shoots the scent but circles back until he finds it again.

Trailing dog misses turn but searches for the scent

Wind

17

MAR dog handler that her dog has detected the scent of a cat. This natural excitement (tail wags, whining, sniffing) is further developed through positive reinforcement training.

There are two advantages to training a cat-detection dog. First, since you are simply reinforcing a natural behavior (excitement for kitties) the dog already exhibits, the training process tends to be rather quick—three to five months. Second, since a cat-detection dog does not require a scent article (something that contains the scent of the lost cat) and since she will alert on any (and every) cat who is in the search area, you can work all lost cat cases, including multi-cat households where there is no clean scent article available. The disadvantage to training a cat-detection dog is that you are restricted to using your search dog only for lost cats.

Best Dogs for the Job

Dogs who have a superior level of excitement to lick and play with cats will excel in this training method. Some of these dogs will chase cats if given the chance. They are often too exuberant to live with a cat because they can't contain their excitement. The key is to select a dog who would never *injure* a cat. This requires a dog who will back down when scratched by a cat. How to properly evaluate a dog for this discipline is covered in Chapter 4.

Cat-detection dog, Susie, plays with target cat, Cheeto.

Trailing Dogs

MAR trailing dogs are specialists in tracking the scent trail of lost dogs. In advanced training, they can be cross-trained to track the scent trail of other animals that can travel great distances, such as horses, ferrets, and even certain cats.

The traditional image of a trailing dog is a Bloodhound, in harness, dragging his handler while on the hot scent of an escaped fugitive. Today, many different breeds are trained in the method of trailing. The MAR trailing dog is trained to follow the trail of scent left behind by a missing animal who has moved out of an area. This will be scent that has drifted in the air, settled onto the ground, and has clung to moist areas, such as gutters, bushes, and vegetation. The scent can become pooled into a cloud of scent in certain areas if the missing pet stayed in one spot long enough and created what is called a "scent pool." The trailing dog may also react to the airborne scent particles and work into the source of the scent should the dog encounter the fresh "air scent" of the missing pet. When this happens, the trailing dog abandons the ground scent, lifts his head as he detects the airborne scent, and drags his handler directly to where the missing pet is located.

Even in lost-person search-and-rescue, trailing dogs hardly ever track right up to the lost person (called a "walk up find"). Yet they often provide critical information such as a direction of travel that can result in other resources making the actual find. Trailing dogs can retrace the path of a missing dog and help develop witnesses who can provide further information. They can provide a direction of travel and help the pet owner know which direction the lost dog initially went, thus aiding in where to place missing-pet posters. In cases where the trailing dog is called out immediately, within hours, there is a good shot of catching up to a missing dog.

On occasion, a trailing dog can be used to search for a cat when the case involves an indoor-only cat who escapes outdoors or when an outdoor cat is displaced into unfamiliar territory (e.g., escaped from a veterinarian's office, involved in a car accident and fled the accident scene). The reason you wouldn't use a trailing dog to search for an outdoor cat who disappears *in his own territory* is that the missing cat's scent will be heavily concentrated in a large scent pool all over the entire search area (*see Diagram 3*), making it extremely difficult to follow a scent trail, which is what trailing dogs are trained to do.

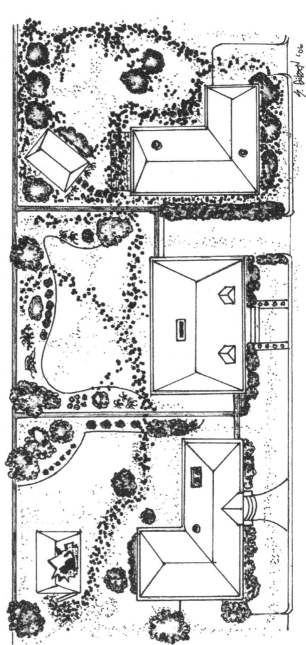

Diagram 3

Scent trail left by the displaced cat. The scent trail has diverged from the footsteps due to dispersment.

Footsteps of the displaced cat.

While a large scent pool is not a problem for a cat-detection dog, it is often too much of a challenge for a trailing dog. On the occasion when a cat is displaced into an unfamiliar area (e.g., indoor-only cat escapes outside, escapes from the vet's office, escapes car after traffic accident), then a trailing dog can effectively pick up the single scent trail, one that starts at the point where the cat escaped (Point A) and ends where the cat is hiding (Point B), *see Diagram 4*.

Diagram 4

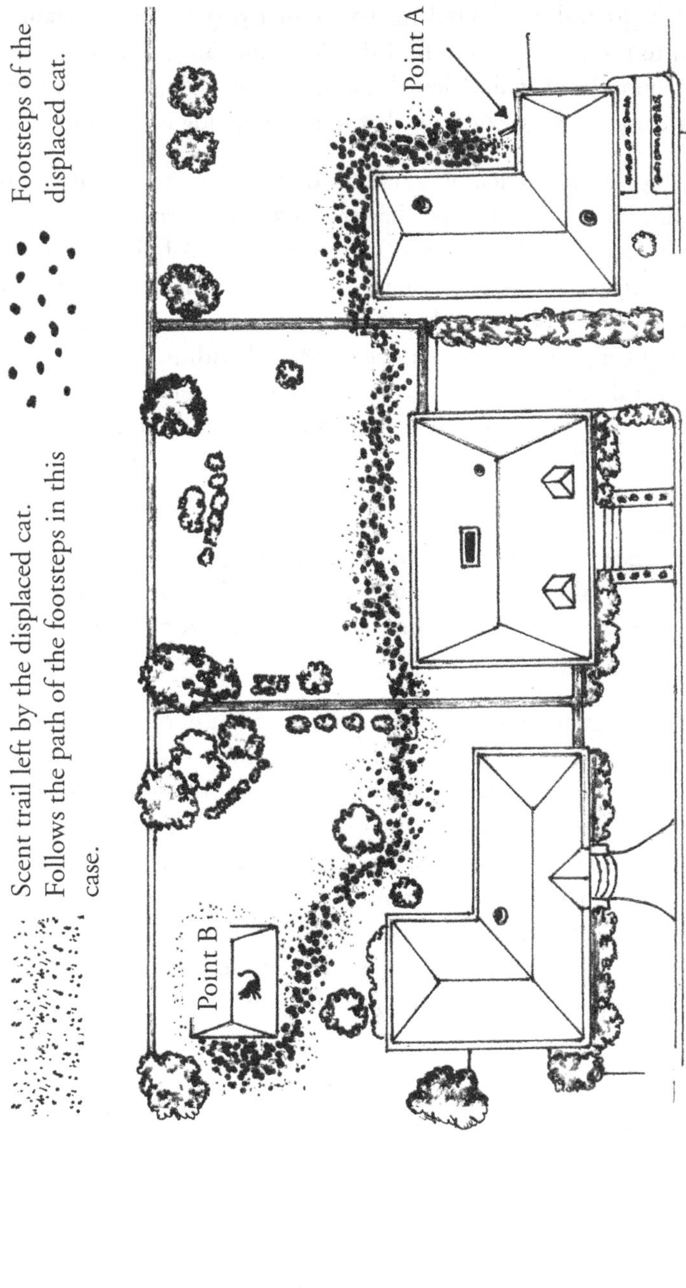

Footsteps of the displaced cat.

Scent trail left by the displaced cat. Follows the path of the footsteps in this case.

Point A

Point B

Training Overview

The trailing dog is presented with a scent article that contains only the scent of the missing pet. The trailing dog is trained to understand that whatever scent is presented to him is the scent that he is to track. The initial training is taught with hide-and-seek games using "target dogs"—other dogs who are trained to run and hide from the trailing dog. This is an exciting game if you have the right dog, one who loves to play with other dogs and can't stand to see another dog run away. Trailing dogs learn to use their noses to find the dog who runs away and hides. After many months of trailing lost dogs, other animals (i.e., cats, ferrets, horses) are used to lay scent trails that the trailing dog is trained to follow.

The biggest advantage of a trailing dog is that she can often establish the direction that a lost pet has traveled, which enables the pet owner to narrow the search area and increases the probability of making a recovery. In many cases, trailing dogs help develop leads from witnesses who previously observed the lost dog, but were not aware that she was a missing pet. Witnesses often come forward with information once they see a pet detective and MAR dog tracking the scent trail hours (or days) later. On rare occasions, trailing dogs may track right up to where a lost pet is located, resulting in an instant reunion between the lost pet and her owner.

The biggest disadvantage of training a trailing dog is the amount of time it takes to train. Because trailing requires teaching advanced skills, it can take twelve to eighteen months to train and certify a dog in this discipline.

Trailing dogs are trained to lock onto the scent of one individual animal as opposed to cat-detection dogs who are trained to detect the scent of all cats in a specific area. This means that if you don't have a scent article—an item that contains the lost pet's scent—the chances of working a successful scent trail with a trailing dog are dramatically reduced. This also means that you'll spend considerable time teaching the dog to ignore the scent of other people, dogs, cats, and other animals while she's working. If she encounters another dog while on the trail of a missing dog, she should not be distracted, but continue on with her work.

Another disadvantage is that working a trailing dog is physically demanding on both dog and handler. Because you are holding onto the end of a long leash, you'll need to go wherever the trailing dog takes you. You'll be at the mercy of where the scent has drifted and settled, which can often be down slopes, up steep terrain, or through thick brush. Missing pets do not travel in straight lines and they do not stick to well-traveled paths. To handle a trailing dog, you must be fit, fearless, and enjoy jogging behind the dog.

Best Dogs for the Job

The best dog to train as a MAR trailing dog is a dog who loves to play with other dogs. A dog who takes an intense interest in other dogs, has a curiosity to use her nose on the ground and follow ground scent, and who goes ballistic when a target dog runs away and hides is an ideal candidate for trailing work.

Dogs who love to play with other dogs make ideal MAR trailing dogs.

Dual-Purpose Dogs

MAR dual-purpose dogs are trained in both area and trailing search methods. If an outdoor cat is lost, these dogs are used (just like cat-detection dogs) in an attempt to detect the scent of *any* cat who is out there. If a dog is lost, these same dogs can be deployed to track the scent trail of a lost dog (or other animal) using scent discrimination trailing techniques (just like trailing dogs) in an attempt to establish a direction of travel. With advanced training, dual-purpose dogs can be used to trail various types of animals such as cats, reptiles, snakes, ferrets, rabbits or larger animals, such as missing horses or livestock.

Training Overview

Dual-purpose dogs are trained to alert on the airborne scent of cats, as well as trail the scent of dogs (and other animals) using the same methods used to train both cat-detection dogs and trailing dogs. Typically, dual-purpose dogs are worked with different equipment and different cues to help them differentiate when they are expected to detect the scent pool of a cat or track the scent trail of a lost dog or other animal. The handler first trains the dual-purpose dog in preliminary trailing work. Once the dog is no longer watching a target dog and is working with a stationary scent article, cat detection training can begin.

The primary advantage of training a dual-purpose dog is you end up with a versatile dog who can search for lost cats, dogs, and various species.

There are two disadvantages to training a dual-purpose dog. First, the pool of potential dual-purpose candidates is limited because it requires a unique dog, one who is excited about both cats and dogs. Second, because you cannot train a dual-purpose dog to ignore the scent of cats, you run the risk of him being distracted by cat scent while tracking the scent of a lost dog. Although you use different cues and equipment for dual-purpose cat detection work and dual-purpose trailing, there's always a chance that the dog's natural excitement (for kitties) will override his training (to stick to the lost dog scent trail).

Best Dogs for the Job

Only dogs who have a superior level of excitement to lick and play with cats and who are hyper-excited to play with other dogs will excel at this training method. Review the "Best Dogs for the Job" descriptions for both cat-detection and trailing dogs and when you find a dog that meets both of these descriptions, you have found a perfect candidate for dual-purpose work.

Right Dog, Right Job

I'm a firm believer in selecting the right dog for the right job. More than likely, you already have a companion dog you hope will be your working partner. However, you owe it to yourself, to your dog, and to the pet owners who are going to rely on your services in the future, to train the best dog possible for the task at hand.

It is entirely possible to train a dog to do this work who is not naturally inclined to seek out/play with cats or other dogs. However, it is considerably more work than simply selecting one who has a natural talent for MAR work. It always makes more sense to engage a dog in a job that he's naturally suited to rather than struggle with convincing him to do something that doesn't turn him on.

Maybe you want to train your dog in cat-detection work, but if your dog isn't nuts about kitties you're probably wasting your time. You need a dog who is either crazy about cats and/or other dogs in order to train a MAR dog who is motivated to search for hours without being distracted or bored. You need a dog who has a readable alert—his body language changes (intense sniffing, rapid tail wiggling, and/or changing directions to zero in on a scent)—so you can tell when he smells something and he's trying hard to find it. If you train a dog with a mediocre drive for these activities you will end up with a mediocre MAR dog, one who will have problems passing a certification test, one who is difficult to read because her alert is subtle, one who will lead a search in the wrong direction, or one who will walk past a cat without alerting because she's too hot, too tired, or too bored.

Finding Other Pets

Occasionally I'm asked how to train a dog to find lost animals other than dogs and cats. These include horses, ferrets, reptiles, and other pets. My experience shows that the two training methods featured in this book, area search and trailing, can be adapted to teach a dog to locate these different species. The scent discrimination method used to teach trailing dogs lends itself to eventually switching to tracking species other than dogs. But if someone wants to train a dog specifically to track lost horses and didn't want to track dogs, she could simply select a dog who loves to play with other dogs, follow the methods in this book, and eventually switch over to using target horses instead of target dogs. In addition to my own dogs, I've seen several former trailing dogs who made an easy transition from tracking human scent to tracking pet scent. It seems that once the dogs learn scent discrimination trailing and the concept of "smell this smell, follow the scent trail of this same smell," they can easily follow scent trails left by horses, ferrets, llamas, and other animals.

The cat-detection training method can also be adapted to train a dog to conduct area searches for species such as snakes, turtles, rabbits, or ferrets. If a ferret fancier owns a dog who becomes excited about ferrets, she could easily train the dog to be a ferret-detection dog using the cat-detection training methods featured in Chapter 9. In addition, a detection dog handler could easily cross-train a dog to search for and detect other species so long as he follows the same cat-detection training techniques (but use a different cue: "snake" or "ferret" instead of the "kitty"). Although the focus of this book is training cat-detection, trailing, and dual-purpose dogs, feel free to adapt the training exercises in this book to help you train your dog to specialize in finding whatever species of animal for which you intend to search.

Tracking vs. Trailing

Many dog enthusiasts are familiar with tracking for sport as it is done under the auspices of the American Kennel Club. It is a fun and popular activity, but there are differences between tracking and MAR trailing work. However, to say that tracking dog and trailing dog handlers differ on how to train a dog to follow a scent trail is an understatement.

First, tracking focuses on the dog and his handler following a scent trail laid by a human. The scent trail forms from a combination of scent particles deposited on crushed vegetation and hard surfaces caused by the weight of the person and motion. Regardless of the source of the scent or the nature of the surface, the dog is expected to work the scent on the track where the person walked. In training and while being tested, tracking dogs are usually penalized, if not disqualified, for straying too far from this track. Much of tracking training involves controlling the dog's movement in order to make certain that the dog remains "on track."

Conversely, the concept behind trailing is that the dog is allowed to work both the track from crushed vegetation or hard surface, as well as airborne scent particles that have drifted and settled to form a cloud or "trail" of scent. With trailing, the dog most often works wherever the scent source is the strongest. Just as in tracking, the dog works in a harness and a long (twenty-foot) lead. Yet in trailing, the handler jogs with the dog wherever the *dog* prefers to work the scent as opposed to where the *handler* thinks the dog should work the scent. The job of the trailing dog handler is to interpret the dog's body language to determine if he still has the scent trail, has switched to another distracting scent, has overshot a turn and lost the scent, has entered a scent pool, or has found the scent cone coming directly from the source of the search.

In addition, trailing involves scent discrimination. Unlike the tracking dog, the trailing dog is presented with a scent article containing the scent of the missing person or pet and will exclusively follow that scent trail. Unlike tracking training, trailing dogs are specifically exposed to several "decoy dogs" during their training to teach them to stay true to a particular scent.

Some trailing dogs work naturally with their noses to the ground and others carry their heads high; some dogs will curl their tail while on the scent and others will stop and shake their body (like dogs do after they've rolled in grass) when they lose the scent. During training, trailing dogs are allowed to overshoot turns, but are eventually *anchored* (slowed down) by their handlers and encouraged to turn around and search for the scent. This enables a handler to read the dog when he is on the scent and to know what he looks like when he loses the scent.

If you have experience training and working tracking dogs, I encourage you to utilize the trailing method outlined in this book to teach your dog to find lost pets. In my experience, the handlers who tried to train a MAR trailing dog by using AKC tracking methods were not as successful in training their dogs to find lost pets as were those who used trailing methods.

Chapter 3
SELECTING A DOG FOR MAR WORK

One of the most critical decisions you'll make in your professional career as a pet detective is selecting a dog to train for MAR work. I'm often asked, "What breed is the best breed to train to look for missing pets?" Many people who ask this question know that I have trained and worked Bloodhounds, and assume that I'd automatically recommend the Bloodhound, but as you will see, many breeds can excel at this work.

Chase, a MAR trailing dog, excels in finding lost pets because she has an intense interest in other dogs, not just because she's a Bloodhound.

When selecting a dog for any type of work, it is always important to consider what they were originally bred to do. It is easier to work with a dog with the right natural instinct than it is to train that instinct into a dog. If you want a dog to follow a scent trail and hunt, a dog bred to hunt will be easier to train than a dog bred to sit on a lap or pull a sled. While there should be some consideration regarding the breed of dog, the dog's drive or willingness to work should be the primary consideration.

Breed Suitability

Area Searches

Hunting dogs, such as the English Pointer, Weimaraner, or German Short-haired Pointer, which are bred to freeze and point, can be ideal breeds to train for area search work. My personal experience using Weimaraners is that when they suddenly discover a hidden cat, they either freeze in place or give off rapid tail wiggles, an alert that is very easy to read. Don't assume that all Weimaraners or all pointing breeds will behave like this. You must evaluate an individual dog's temperament and drive, and make a selection based on how she behaves, not on breed alone.

Small breeds offer certain advantages when searching for cats. Terriers or small spaniels have an advantage over larger breeds because they can crawl underneath houses, decks, and porches. I've had good luck using terriers (e.g., Jack Russell, Cairn) as cat detection dogs because of their small size and their instinct to focus on critters. Flat-faced breeds or dogs with short muzzles—a condition known as "brachycephalic"—should be avoided. This includes breeds the Pug, Pekingese, and Bulldog, which have difficulty breathing due to the lack of a snout. Recruiting these breeds for scent work, especially in warmer weather, is probably not a wise move.

Some breeds simply do not lend themselves to area search work. If you plan to search for missing cats, for example, there are breeds you should avoid. While a Greyhound or Saluki might have a keen interest in cats, I hesitate to recommend one of these breeds for fear that their instinct to chase small prey—the purpose for which they were originally bred—might cause them to take off in hot pursuit of the cat. Obviously, the goal is to locate and protect a missing pet, not chase him down and capture or injure him!

Trailing

My personal preference for breeds to use in trailing work includes hounds, such as Bloodhounds, and hunting breeds, such as Labrador Retrievers and Golden Retrievers. German Shepherds and Border Collies have proven themselves in various forms of search work and should also be considered. If the terrain you will be searching includes ticks, foxtails and stickers, or extreme heat, consider a short-coated breed. On the other hand, if you will be searching in cold climates, consider a thick-coated breed. Never rule out a mixed-breed dog as long as her drive and temperament are conducive to MAR work. A perfect example of a great mixed-breed trailing dog is Sonja, an Akita mix, that I trained. Sonja was rescued from a life of guard-dog duty (she was permanently tied to a tree in a backyard and starved for attention) and has done a fantastic job in her initial training.

Sonja, a mixed-breed MAR trailing dog, has done well in trailing because she loves to play with other dogs.

Trailing work is not appropriate for many breeds, such as Chihuahuas, Chows, or Shih Tzus. A trailing dog must cover great distances, especially if you are tracking a dog missing in the wilderness. Small breeds, lap dogs, and dogs of massive size (e.g., Great Dane, St. Bernard) make poor trailing candidates due to the physical demands of the work.

Breed preference is exactly that—a preference. I've seen a Golden Retriever named Kea who could out-track any Bloodhound. The reason this particular dog was so successful was a combination of her love for people, an extremely high level of drive, and a knowledgeable handler who learned how to both train and trust her dog. (The story of Kea and how she found my Bloodhound, A.J., is mentioned in the Introduction.) One of the misconceptions about MAR dogs is the assumption that a certain breed can perform the task at hand simply because it was bred for the work. Do not make the mistake of believing that just because you have selected a hound, your dog will automatically trail or just because you selected a pointer, your dog will automatically point.

The Importance of Drive

While selecting an appropriate breed (or mixed breed) is important, the dog must exhibit the proper drive to seek out the type of pet for which you are searching. For cat detection work, the dog should have an intense drive for cats. Dogs who love to play with cats, perhaps even chase them (without hurting them) and who give a dramatic physical response when they first detect the scent of a cat are good candidates. For trailing work, you want a dog who *loves* to play with other dogs and who goes crazy when another dog runs away and hides. For dual-purpose work you want a dog that combines both drives, exhibits a desire to play with and/or chase both cats and other dogs.

Traits and Temperament

When selecting a dog for any type of search work, there are certain traits and temperaments that you should favor, and certain traits and temperaments you should avoid:

What to look for

- A dog who is healthy
- A dog who is easily motivated by food, clicker training, or toys
- A dog who is highly excited about cats or other dogs/pets
- A dog who is fearless in new environments and confident with strange people, locations, and noises
- A dog who is obedient, willing to listen, and will obey when there are distractions
- A dog who can be left in a crate and relaxes when left alone

What to avoid

- A dog who is unfriendly toward strangers

- A dog who is aggressive toward other dogs

- A dog who has killed or injured a cat or another animal

- A dog who has an aversion to certain types of people (does not like men with beards, is afraid of people wearing hats, etc.)

- A dog who has significant health problems

- A dog who is afraid of traffic, machinery, strange objects, thunder, or anything that you might encounter during a search

- A dog who is uncontrollable when off lead

- A dog who ignores you, refuses to come when called

- A dog who has a fear of crawling in cramped spaces, such as under a porch, deck, or house

Age Considerations

A common question is whether or not an older dog can be trained and used as a MAR dog. This is more of a personal decision and is not as crucial as the drive and temperament of the dog.

In selecting and training traditional search-and-rescue dogs, age is a major consideration. Because it takes an average of two years to train and certify a traditional search dog, starting a dog above the age of three is typically discouraged. This is primarily because the amount of time, energy and finances that need to be invested in training a traditional search-and-rescue dog would be wasted if the dog were only physically able to perform for a few years. Most handlers in traditional search-and-rescue prefer to start with either a puppy or a dog who is about one year old.

There are slightly different issues regarding age when considering training a dog for MAR work. Training a dog who is mature and has an established temperament and drive can be an advantage over training a puppy whose suitability for the work is still uncertain. What if you selected an eight-week-old puppy to train for MAR only to find out that in four months, she is dog-aggressive, afraid of cats, or has no interest in working for you? You are safer starting with a dog who is at least six to eight months old or older. By picking a more mature dog, you will have a better idea of any defects in the dog's temperament or drive.

If you have a dog who is older (five to nine years old) that you believe would take to MAR training with ease, understand that you might only have a few years of work out of this dog before retirement. Search work is physically demanding, so be sure to select a dog who is physically capable of doing the work.

Chapter 4
MAR Dog
Evaluation Process

The evaluation process is designed to identify which (if any) of the three MAR disciplines your dog is suited for: cat detection, trailing, or dual purpose. While you may have selected a dog who appears to have the proper characteristics, this process will help weed out dogs who are aggressive, extremely fearful, or sensitive to sounds and situations, and weed out dogs who lack the intense drive that is required to train them to be successful dog detectives.

Missing Pet Partnership uses a seven-part evaluation to determine the ability of a dog to perform MAR work. Every dog we evaluate is different and unique. Some dogs fail the evaluation process entirely while others qualify to be trained for all three disciplines. The evaluation has proven to be an effective tool in determining whether or not a dog is suitable for MAR work and, if he is suitable, which of the three disciplines his handler should pursue. Refer to the Resources section to see a full evaluation sheet. The following section will dissect the seven categories in the evaluation, and explain how to test a dog for each of these categories.

Evaluation Categories
The evaluation process tests the prospective MAR dog in seven categories. These are:

- Recall

- Fear
- Human aggression
- Dog aggression
- Dog interest
- Cat interest
- Cat aggression

Recall

A mild distraction is brought nearby the dog while he is in a sit/down stay or held by an assistant; the dog is on lead. The handler calls the dog and the dog ignores the distraction and returns to the handler. The dog must demonstrate a reliable recall without the handler pulling on the lead. The recall evaluation is designed to make sure the MAR dog will come when called by her handler. Dogs who totally ignore their handlers fail this portion of the test.

Fear

The dog is exposed to a clanging noise (lid dropped on a pan), a sudden opening of an umbrella, banging of spoon on a pan, and/or banging of crutches or broom on the ground. Dog must not show an excessive level of fear.

Because they must be capable of working in various environments, such as noisy construction sites, busy shopping centers, and natural disaster zones, MAR dogs must be fearless, capable of putting up with weird sights, loud sounds, and strange people. Dogs who are clearly stressed and afraid do not pass this portion of the test. An initial startle response to the noise/stimuli is expected. However, if the dog continues to back away or hide behind his handler and does not adapt to the noise/stimuli, he is probably not suitable for MAR work.

Human Aggression

A person unknown to the dog approaches him and acts strangely: waves his arms, staggers, or wears a hat, an overcoat, or garbage bag with his head poking out. The stranger moves within a few feet of the dog and stares directly at him with crutches or a broom held overhead in a threatening manner. The dog must not show excessive fear or aggression. The preferred response is friendly tail-wagging, looking away, and other submissive body language.

MAR candidates should be evaluated for any aggression toward humans by exposing them to people who are acting strangely.

MAR dogs must be friendly toward people, other dogs, and cats. A dog who cannot be trusted around people or animals is potential trouble. MAR dogs should be capable of being in a crowd of children who want to pet him, controllable when a stray dog approaches, and trusted that they won't injure a cat if one bolts from a hiding place during a search. Dogs who fail this portion of the test are dogs who are clearly panicked or become aggressive. A dog who barks while backing up is acceptable since this can be a sign of a dog who is afraid (but not to the point of panic) and is being protective. However, a dog who madly struggles and squirms to get away because she is overly panicked is not acceptable. A dog who lunges and snaps, and shows clear signs of aggression is also unacceptable.

Dog Aggression

A "target" dog on a lead approaches the test dog. The target dog should be a friendly, submissive dog who gives off play signals. The dog being tested should not show aggression (growling, barking, snapping, lunging, or raised hackles) toward the strange dog.

It is common to encounter loose, stray dogs during MAR searches or when training in public. All MAR dogs should be friendly and trustworthy around other dogs. Dogs who give off dominate signals (hackles raised, stiff approach, staring, placing head over shoulder of other dog) can easily trigger another dominant dog to fight. Dogs who fail this portion of the test are dogs who growl, snap, lunge or attempt to pick a fight with a strange, submissive dog.

Dog Interest

A target dog on lead approaches the MAR dog, who is attached to 30-foot lead, and invites him to play. The MAR dog should wag his tail and focus intently on the target dog. The MAR dog's body might dip into a play bow so that his body language makes it clear that he wants to play. The target dog should be allowed to come up and play with the MAR dog. Both dogs should interact, preferably they will play. Then the target dog's handler will suddenly sprint away with the dog and hide. The MAR dog should focus on the target dog. Desired behaviors are whining, jumping, barking, pulling, and even hysterical behavior because the target dog ran away. Acceptable MAR dog behaviors are ears perked and eyes focused on the target dog. As soon as the target dog is hidden from view, the MAR dog handler releases the collar of the MAR dog (but continues to hold onto the end of the thirty-foot lead). Ideally, the MAR dog should pull the handler and race around the corner to find and play with the target dog.

The dog attraction evaluation tests suitability for MAR trailing dog work. The basis of training a MAR trailing dog is hide-and-seek games known as runaway exercises. Dogs who excel in this work are dogs who become frantic and hysterical with excitement when another dog runs away and hides. Dogs who are not suited for this work and who fail this portion of the evaluation are dogs who don't care when another dog runs away and hides. Other dogs who fail this portion of the evaluation are dogs who, when released, do not run straight for the hidden target dog, but are instead distracted or find something more interesting to them. Just like sled dogs, the job of a MAR trailing dog is to *pull* into their harness. Dogs who hesitate to pull hard into the leash or to run ahead of their handler (perhaps because they have had a lot of heeling training) might not be suitable for MAR trailing work. The ideal dog is one who will drag their handler on a scent trail—willing to ignore previous anti-pulling training—because they are so driven to follow another dog and, frankly, nothing else at that moment matters.

Potential trailing dogs should be extremely excited when another dog runs away.

Cat Interest

For these tests, use a "target" cat who is not afraid of dogs and who will not hiss, spit, swat, or bite a dog. It is critical that you use a target cat who enjoys dogs and will not create a bad experience for the dog being tested. The test dog is walked up to a concealed, crated feline. The handler should be silent and should not attempt to lead the dog (unless instructed) to the cat. The dog should show enough interest in the cat scent that she moves toward it to investigate. The dog must show a physical reaction (tail wag, fixation, whining, etc.) indicating strong interest and should remain focused on the crate. The dog should not show an aversion or fear of the cat (which a majority of dogs show).

The cat-interest evaluation tests suitability for MAR cat-detection work. The basis of training a cat-detection dog is to hide a crated target cat, then allow the dog to find, and sometimes play with that cat. To accurately test a potential cat-detection dog, the target cat should not be visible to the dog. This can be accomplished in three ways: 1) the cat can be placed inside of a plastic cat carrier and totally concealed within bushes; 2) the cat can be placed inside a plastic cat carrier in total darkness and dog's reaction is observed by flashlight; or 3) the cat can be placed inside a cloth mesh cat carrier (I recommend the Sherpa brand bag) that looks more like a black suitcase than it does an animal cage. The purpose of concealing the carrier is to observe the reaction of the dog when she encounters the airborne scent of a cat. The initial response is typically what you see when the dog encounters cat scent on an actual search.

Use a black cloth mesh cat carrier to conceal the target cat when evaluating and training MAR cat-detection dogs.

Dogs who fail the cat-interest evaluation will show an aversion to the target cat by backing away or otherwise showing fear. Dogs who show an excessive amount of excitement (lunge at the carrier, snap and bark, or clearly want to "get" the kitty to harm him) are also not suitable for cat-detection work. Dogs who pass the evaluation for cat detection work are dogs who respond with controlled excitement, which can include frantic tail wagging, whining, and a fascination with the cat. In most cases, these are dogs who have had good experiences with cats; they may even live with a kitty.

It can be risky to evaluate a dog who has an unknown history with cats. Extreme caution should be used to determine if the dog's excitement is because he wants to play with the cat or if he wants to hurt the cat.

Cat Aggression

The purpose of the cat-aggression test is to further confirm that the dog's interest in cats is benign: lick, groom, or play, never bite or injure a cat. This section of the test should be performed only with dogs who have a confirmed history of getting along with cats and who have passed the cat interest evaluation. The target cat must enjoy dogs and since you will remove the cat from the carrier, it is important that you take precautions to protect him. This test should be performed carefully, and the target cat and the dog should wear a harness attached to a long lead.

For this test, an unfamiliar cat is walked near the restrained dog. The dog shows excitement and friendly interest, but no aggression toward the cat. The dog, on a long lead, is allowed to sniff and approach the cat, but does not snap, lunge, or attempt to hurt the cat. The dog should be fixated on the cat and undistracted.

Initially, the dog is at least five feet away and is not allowed to reach the cat. Allow the cat to walk naturally out of the crate as you observe the dog's reaction. Slowly allow the dog to advance toward the cat's hindquarters. Do not let the dog first approach the cat's face when introducing the two because this is inviting the cat to slap the dog and the dog to react by biting.

Once the dog reaches the cat's hindquarters, allow him to sniff. The dog should sniff, nuzzle, maybe even lick. Praise him as he sniffs and enjoys the cat. If he is under control, slowly allow him to investigate the cat. Be prepared to pull him back and make sure the target-cat handler is prepared to pull the cat away should the animals act aggressively. Keep your hand near the dog's muzzle so you can stop any attempts to bite.

Slowly allow the test dog to advance toward the cat's hindquarters.

If the dog bites at the cat, you have a dog who could present a real problem. Nibbling, like how dogs chatter their teeth on something furry, is acceptable but nipping and biting is not. Only dogs who can be trusted fully with cats can be used in cat-detection work.

Magnets and Targets

Not every dog is suitable for MAR work. If you (and your dog) wish to participate in the field, there are two other jobs that may be suitable. *Magnet* dogs play a key role in helping to attract loose pets, and *target* dogs are used in training.

Magnet Dogs

Magnet dogs are very (overly) friendly dogs used to capture panicked, stray dogs who are afraid to come to people. While not trained to find lost pets, the natural friendliness of the magnet dog is used to attract a loose dog who otherwise would be too afraid to be captured once he is spotted by a pet detective or whose location has been pinpointed by a MAR dog. Magnet dogs are especially useful for cases in which a skittish, shy dog runs from everyone, including her owner.

Once the magnet-dog handler (usually a MAR technician) spots the loose dog, he brings out the magnet dog, who is wearing a harness attached to a thirty-foot lead. The handler holds the lead in one hand and a Snappy

Snare (an animal capturing tool) in the other. The magnet dog is allowed to entice and distract the loose dog while the handler lets out the lead to put distance between himself and the two dogs. As the dogs greet and sniff each other and the loose dog becomes more comfortable, the magnet dog handler moves closer to the loose dog. He quickly slips the snare over the loose dog's neck and captures him. This technique, also known as "attract-and-capture," is explained and demonstrated in the Missing Pet Partnership MAR Technician Course. It is a highly effective method to recover skittish dogs because one of the dog's strongest instincts is the pack instinct. Panicked dogs often approach another dog before they approach a person.

While magnet dog Kody attracts and distracts a loose dog, her handler prepares to use a Snappy Snare to capture the stray.

Target Dogs

A target dog is the second type of non-search dog job that is available within MAR work. Target dogs are used to help train MAR trailing dogs by laying a scent trail. Laying a trail involves a target-dog handler taking her dog for a walk. As a target dog walks, his scent leaves a trail to be followed by the trailing dog. However, before the target dog lays the scent trail, the handler collects scent from the target dog by rubbing a sterile gauze pad over the face, ears, tummy, and/or near the anal glands. Once the target dog lays the trail, the handler presents the gauze pad to the MAR trailing dog. The MAR trailing dog sniffs the gauze pad, follows the matching scent trail, and finds the hidden target dog.

Target dogs are dog-friendly dogs who are used to lay a scent trail by simply going for a walk with a handler.

Target dogs must be friendly dogs who love playing with other dogs. The primary goal of a target dog is to create a positive experience for the MAR trailing dog. The trailing dog learns that it is fun and rewarding to track and find another dog.

Target Cats

There are roles for cats to play in the MAR process, as well. Target cats are used to train both MAR cat-detection and dual-purpose dogs. In general, these are gregarious, bold kitties who have no fear of dogs. Target cats do not mind being nuzzled, licked, and nibbled on by an exuberant dog. These cats might even approach a strange dog or, at the very least, they will not exhibit fear when a new dog approaches.

Access to a target cat is critical when training a dog to locate lost cats. If you do not own a cat of your own, find someone in your area who owns a gregarious cat who is willing to train her to be a target cat.

Target cats are taught to wear a harness and lead, to be comfortable with traveling, and to sit quietly in a crate when hidden from cat-detection dogs and dual-purpose dogs. Although you eventually condition the dog to listen for a cat's meow, the initial training is focused on teaching the dog to use his sense of smell to find where the cat is hiding.

Teaching a target cat to wear a harness takes time. Choose a harness that will not be easy for the cat to squirm out of. I prefer an adjustable, small-dog harness made of one-eighth inch wide, nylon web with a plastic buckle that snaps in place. Cats seem less likely to slip out of these dog harnesses than cat harnesses of thinner width. Place the harness on the cat before you feed him canned food or give him a special treat to condition him to tolerate the harness. If the cat is an indoor-only cat who yearns to go outdoors, he can learn to enjoy, or at least tolerate the harness if he associates it with going outside.

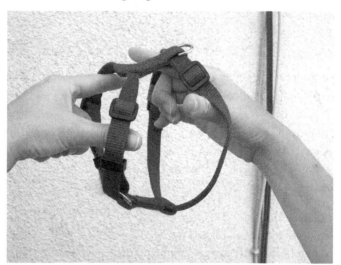

Target cats should wear adjustable, small, web harnesses that are difficult to slip out of.

The target cat will get used to traveling if you take him places on a regular basis. Initially, he might be afraid and reluctant, but taking him along for a ride in the car and combining this with something pleasant will condition him to relax in the crate. If your cat only associates the crate with a trip to the veterinarian, you may have some difficulties to overcome.

The easiest and most effective way to train a target cat to sit quietly in a crate involves feeding wild birds. This training technique should only be used during comfortable weather—never when it is too hot or too cold. Set up a bird and/or squirrel feeding station with bird seed and water. Set an empty crate about ten feet away from the food so the wildlife becomes accustomed to the crate. Once you've successfully attracted birds and/or squirrels to come to the feeding station, place the cat inside the crate.

Target cats quickly learn to be quiet once the squirrels and birds arrive. Their hunting instincts kick in and they do not meow because it frightens away the potential "prey." Target cats associate being in crates as something enjoyable and they learn that being silent produces more wildlife. Before you know it, the target cat is sleeping in his crate at home, a not-so-subtle hint that he wants to go outside for more bird watching! Access to two or three different target cats ensures that a cat-detection dog learns to find any and every cat that he encounters. If you train only with one cat, you run the risk that the dog alerts only for a particular cat. Network with feline fanciers to build up your access to several target cats.

Chapter 5
SCENT

The more familiar you are with scent concepts—how scent is dispersed, how it is impacted by the environment, how a scent article works and more—the more effective you will be working with MAR dogs. While an extended treatise on scent is beyond the scope of this book, the information included in this chapter will introduce you to the basic concepts you need to learn to work in this field. I certainly do not claim to be an authority on the topic of scent. There is so much that is simply not known or understood about it. See the Resources for further reading suggestions.

Scent Dispersal

Most of the research on scent dispersal has focused on humans. However, the same principles apply to animals, so the following information applies to MAR work. Scent is dispersed from a body in several ways, from both internal and external sources. A human body is made up of trillions of cells, all of which have a definite life span[1] (see footnotes at end of chapter). The most common definition of scent is that it is bacteria acting upon shed (dead) skin and respiratory cells.[2] The most common external form of scent dispersal is from the constant shedding of skin cells.

Skin cells usually live as healthy skin for about thirty-six hours before they are shed, while cells in the intestines last about forty hours. Approximately fifty-million cells die every second and are eventually dispersed from our bodies.[3] Dead skin cells known as "rafts" flake off from the body and are dispersed by floating in the air or by being rubbed off by coming into contact with something. If the cells are clumped together, they may drift only a short distance. If there is very low or no wind present, skin cells may float down and land a short distance from where the person or animal walked or stood. If the rafts are light and there is a heavy wind, they may be carried a great distance before they eventually land.[4] Depending on the weather conditions, the scent that is generated (due to bacterial action) from these shed cells can last for several days.

The area where the airborne scent particles drift and are detectable by a dog is known as a *scent cone*. It is called a cone because the area is small when close to the source of the scent, but fans out creating a cone-shaped area the farther it is dispersed. The immediate area surrounding where a cloud of scent hovers is known as a "scent pool." Just like the *Peanuts* character Pig Pen, humans and animals disperse clouds of scent that surround them when they are still. The longer that humans and animals remain in one place, the larger this pool of scent grows. A scent pool can remain intact even after the source of scent has moved on. Thus, a cat may crouch in one location and create a large scent pool, bolt and run to a new location, and a cat-detection dog would still alert to the large scent pool before it dissipates. The rate that a scent pool dissipates depends upon the terrain, temperature, and wind conditions.

Sometimes weather conditions will cause scent to hover close to the ground and dissipate outward over a vast area rather than upward into the atmosphere. Temperature inversions are created by variable temperatures that trap scent and other particles, such as pollutants and smoke, and either hold them high above the ground or close to it. Warm air rises and cold air falls, so on warmer days the inversion layer is high, above the tree tops, and on cold, winter days the layer is close to the ground. You can actually see inversion layers when, for example, on a hot summer day smoke from a large forest fire is trapped at a high altitude as it is dispersed over a large area. On the other hand, smoke from a campfire on a brisk, cold morning can be seen hovering closer to the ground as it is dispersed laterally.

A natural gas leak wreaked havoc in New York City on January 7, 2007, on a damp, rainy day. The smell of methyl mercaptan, the chemical component added to natural gas to give it the odor of rotten eggs, was detected as far north as Central Park and as far south as Jersey City. Nineteen people were sent to the hospital and reportedly 409 fire trucks scrambled to investigate the fumes. Various news sources reported that a construction-related natural gas leak occurred at 10th and Bleecker Streets, but New York City Mayor Michael Bloomberg stated in a press conference that the Bleecker Street leak, "could not account for the widespread smell." Authorities were perplexed as to how the odor of natural gas was detected over such a large area. During the incident, speculation of terrorist involvement grew as did the media coverage. But no other source of the odor was found and after a period of several hours; the giant scent cloud finally dispersed from the area.

The natural gas that escaped from the broken gas main at 10th and Bleecker was likely trapped under an inversion layer. In fact, later that evening a meteorologist reported that due to a warm front that had covered the city that morning, it was very possible that a temperature inversion had pushed the gas from the site of the Bleecker gas leak closer to the ground. Since the air (and gas) could not rise, it simply hovered and remained low to the ground as it slowly dispersed out of the area. If that same gas leak had taken place on a day when there was no inversion layer, the scent cloud at the corner of 10th and Bleecker would have probably risen and the story never would have made national news.

How Long Can Scent Survive?

After scent is shed from a human or animal, how long does it survive? The answer to that question is probably one of the hottest topics debated within the search and-rescue and MAR dog field. There are many factors that will affect how long scent remains. Environmental factors such as temperature, wind, humidity and the location of the scent are the biggest factors that can affect how long scent survives.[5]

The ideal conditions for working a trailing dog are cool, moist days with no wind. Scent will pool, cling, and survive in shady areas and areas with lush vegetation. The moisture provided by lush green grass, the shade of a front porch, or the damp surface of a gutter, are all examples of where residual scent can be present several days after the source of the scent has passed through the area. Scent survives longer in cooler conditions, such as in the evening or early morning hours, because lower temperatures tend to bring the scent down to ground level.

Hot and dry conditions have a negative impact on scent survival. In these conditions, scent is more easily dispersed and destroyed. Direct sunlight will dry out and can quickly destroy scent vapors. In addition to the physical toll that it can take on a trailing dog, heat can also cause scent to rise above the level of where the dog is working.[6] Avoid working a search dog in hot temperatures if you can.

This principle of waiting until it is cooler before you work a dog can be difficult to follow if a family member or close friend calls you to say he just lost his dog a few hours ago. I once responded in 100-degree weather to track my pastor's lost dog only to have my Bloodhound, Chase, fail. She was virtually unable to establish a direction of travel because an inversion layer caused by the high temperatures had caused the scent to rise above her head. She picked up some scent in the shade, but she was useless on the hot sidewalks. The worst part was that she was eleven years old and she overheated—something that could have been avoided had I stuck to my guns and waited to respond until the following morning when it was cool and the scent was close to the ground. But telling someone who is close to you and who is frantic that he needs to wait another day before you can respond is not easy to do! Thankfully, the dog was found a few hours later, and Chase recovered from the heat.

Wind can disperse scent great distances, minimizing a scent trail, thus making trailing difficult. In a case where a lost person walked on a sidewalk four days prior to a search, the trailing dog might work very well by dipping down into the driveways, up to front porches of homes, rather than the spot where the person walked on the sidewalk four days prior. If there is grass next to the sidewalk, then the trailing dog might work the grass. The chances of scent remaining directly on pavement are slim after a four-day period. But the chance of scent surviving by clinging to the moisture provided on the grass and in the shady areas is very likely.

Humidity and moisture are vital for bacterial action. According to William Syrotuck, author of *Scent and the Scenting Dog*, moisture "serves as a solvent for food, carries waste products from the bacterial cell, is influential in most chemical activities, forms the major portion of the protoplasm and also acts as a catalyst."[7] The optimal time to work search dogs is when there is no wind and when it is damp, foggy, drizzling, or even raining. I've had many successful training sessions and three walk-up finds (one suicidal man and two different missing cats) that my dogs conducted during moderate to heavy rain. Scent needs moisture to survive, which rain provides. Rain does not make scent mysteriously disappear. Rain will not destroy scent, but a heavy downpour on pavement can disperse it, making it difficult to follow a trail. In those cases, the scent will cling in gutters and puddles instead of being dispersed along a consistent path like a sidewalk.

Scent needs moisture to survive.

So how long can scent survive? The odor of decomposition has been known to change the composition of soil and can be detected by search dogs many years after the body decomposed down to skeletal remains.[8] How long can airborne skunk odor survive once it comes into contact with clothing? Unfortunately, from my experience, skunk odor can remain for quite a long time! (I personally believe that our scent [and animal scent] is as pungent, as strong, and as detectable to a dog as skunk odor is to us.)

For obvious reasons, the longer you wait to work a scent trail, the less likely the dog will work the scent trail successfully. When tracking lost dogs, the longer you wait to respond, the more likely the dog will have moved or been transported a great distance. Thus, the fact that the scent of the missing dog might still be present after seven days is sometimes a moot point if the dog has already traveled twenty miles and you aren't able to catch up to her. This is why Missing Pet Partnership is pushing for *community-based* lost pet services. Ultimately, we want to see the rapid response of MAR trailing dogs who can respond quickly (within hours or a few days) to search for lost dogs in their own community.

Unfortunately, it might take a few days before pet owners learn about your pet detective services. Since you'll often be called out to work scent trails that are three to seven days old, the majority of your training should focus on trails that are aged this long. You should also train the dog on scent trails that are up to two weeks old to learn the dog's limitations when working older trails. Keep in mind that a two-week-old scent trail laid in a residential area that is highly contaminated with other animal scents and dispersed with vehicular traffic is much more difficult to work than a two-week-old scent trail laid in the depths of a cool, damp forest thick with vegetation. Scent has a better chance of surviving in shady, damp, and cool areas than it does in open ground or pavement where it is easily moved by wind currents, swirled around by passing cars, and ultimately dried out and destroyed by direct sunlight.

Although no one knows exactly how many days a scent trail is viable, we *can* make estimates based on prior successes of cases worked by police Bloodhounds and search-and-rescue trailing dogs who have made actual walk-up finds. The *majority* of successful scent trails in which the dogs actually found the lost person or criminal were hours or a few days old. Personally, the oldest "finds" that my trailing dogs have made are in the three- to five-day range. The oldest, documented scent trail that I found in my research is detailed in the book, *The Complete Bloodhound*, by Catherine Brey and Lena Reed. The authors write about how "a new record in man trailing was established" when a Bloodhound handler named Norman Wilson and his three Bloodhounds (Doc Holiday, Queen Guinevere, and Big Nose Kate) successfully tracked a scent trail of three missing people lost in the "wet, dense forests of Western Oregon." By the time Wilson worked his hounds, the scent trail was 322 hours (thirteen days) old. His hounds led Wilson to the bodies of the missing hikers.[9]

I recently contacted police Bloodhound handler/trainer Jeff Schettler and asked him to share his thoughts on how long scent survives. Schettler is highly respected in the Bloodhound community, and has served as a K-9 trainer for numerous law enforcement agencies. Here is what Schettler wrote (in an e-mail to me) about his perspective on how long scent can survive:

The simple fact of the matter is that scent degrades with age and cir-
cumstance. Everything environmental and man-made has an effect on
scent. Because of my job as a K-9 handler, I documented everything I
did in great detail. Everything from the time and date to the weather
conditions was written down. I discovered that the best time to run a
Bloodhound on a trail was a case one to six hours old. If I had a good
scent article and a location to start where the subject was known to have
been, we ran successful trails over 47 percent of the time. By successful,
I mean a trail that ended with a subject in hand, physical evidence, or
witness corroborated statements. Forty-seven percent is a pretty good
number considering all the factors that go into trailing work.

Trails that were over six hours old degenerated in success rate exponen-
tially. There seemed to neither be little rhyme nor reason to the quality
of the trail at this point. Our averages dropped off to the low thirty
percentile. Once our trails aged over twelve to twenty-four hours, success dropped off to the teens and worse. Over twenty-four hours and
I could count the quantity of walk-up finds of people on one hand. In
an urban environment, there are far too many variables involved with
aged trails to ever be able to accurately predict how a dog will work.[10]

I've heard of tracking authorities who believe that a scent trail vanishes
once a person walks on pavement, and others who believe that a scent
trail dissipates after eight hours. At the other end of the spectrum, there
are currently a few pet detectives who claim their search dogs can track a
lost-pet scent trail that is several (five) months old. There is even someone who claims a dog can track a lost-pet scent trail that is up to a year
old! For decades, trailing dogs handled by volunteers and law enforcement officers have only been capable of following scent trails that are *less
than two weeks old* and yet suddenly, people charging a fee for their pet
tracking services are miraculously able to train dogs who can track scent
trails that are months old. While making such claims opens the door for
more business revenues (it enables them to respond on searches where
the lost dog has been missing for months), these type of exaggerated and
unethical claims put MAR work and the pet detective industry in jeop-
ardy of being dismissed as "a scam" by scent-dog professionals who know
better and who understand the fragile nature of scent.

I've spent eighteen years training and working search dogs, observing
other search dogs in training, and in learning from search dog authorities
across the country. I'm familiar with aged-trail experiments performed
by experienced Bloodhound trainers. Based on my knowledge of what

other credible Bloodhound handlers have worked, my training through the National Police Bloodhound Association (NPBA), and my personal experience in working successful cases where search dogs who I've personally trained and/or worked actually made a find, I'm comfortable in estimating that in optimal scent conditions (cool, damp areas with heavy vegetation and no wind) a trained trailing dog is capable of following a scent trail that is up to two (maybe three) weeks old. Any pet detective who claims that a search dog can track a scent trail that is much older than this, especially if they're charging a fee for their services, *should be treated with skepticism.*

To What Extent Can Dogs Detect Scent?

Dogs have an incredible sense of smell. Nearly one-eighth of a dog's brain and over fifty percent of the internal components of a dog's nose are devoted to processing smell (olfaction)[11]. Humans have a much smaller area of olfactory cells. The human nose may contain only about five million sensory cells. In comparison, a large breed dog can have up to 220 million sensory cells in his nose.[12]

A large breed dog can have up to 220 million sensory cells in his nose.

Canine behaviorist Leon Whitney, D.V.M., author of *Dog Psychology: The Basis of Dog Training*, describes just how powerful a dog's nose can be. "We are told that ordinary salt is odorless. Salt in solution is odorless to a man.

Yet dogs can smell it down to a teaspoonful in 13 gallons of water. A teaspoon of acetic acid in 1300 gallons of water (1:1,000,000) is recognized by an ordinary dog. Sulphuric acid, he can smell at 1:10,000,000."[13]

In the mid 1990s, Duane Pickel, a retired police dog handler in Florida trained his Schnauzer, George, to detect melanoma (cancer) cells.[14] Duane worked with a medical facility and proved that George could accurately alert on the presence of melanoma cells. George was even credited with saving the life of a person with a suspicious mole. He alerted and indicated that the mole was cancerous, though the doctor who initially examined the tissue said that it was not. Upon further urging due to the dog's alert, the doctor probed deeper into the tissue and discovered the beginning stages of skin cancer. The story of George's work is incredible when you consider that he was detecting changes in the composition of cells. Today, cancer detection dogs are being trained through various medical research programs.

In my own work using dogs to locate missing snakes, I've known people who are skeptical that a snake gives off scent. Snakes give off pheromones. In order for a snake to mate, it needs to be able to find another snake. The U.S. Department of Agriculture currently uses "snake-detection dogs" specifically trained to sniff out the destructive brown tree snake in an effort to prevent them from accidentally being exported out of Guam. My first experience seeing dogs respond to snake scent was when I witnessed a "snake-avoidance training" session where SAR dogs were brought into the scent cone of a rattlesnake and were corrected if they approached the snake. Six months later, I attended a follow-up session and watched these same dogs react with fear when they were led into the scent cone of a rattlesnake. Just because *we* cannot smell snakes does not mean they do not give off a detectable scent

My dog, Rachel, used to alert while seated next to me whenever I'd get within two blocks of my mother's house (which was three hours from where I lived). She'd be curled up and asleep until she picked up on the large scent pool that was created by my mother living at one location and continuously depositing her scent both inside and outside her house. I know that Rachel picked up this scent coming through the ventilation of my truck as she'd always jut her nose up to the vent and inhale deeply when we were within two blocks of my mother's home. As soon as she detected the scent, Rachel would stand up, shake off, look over at me, whine, and wag her tail. I always watched her out of the corner of my eye, never turning my head or doing anything physically to cue her.

To test my theory that she picked up the scent and was responding to visual cues as we arrived in town, I approached the house from several different directions. My mother's house was located in a residential area with four different possible entrance points. Upon using all four-entrance points, I always encountered the same alert by Rachel. In three of the four cases, she was asleep until two blocks from my mother's home, at which point she woke up and sniffed the incoming air from the vent before she ever looked at me. Her focus was on scent coming in from the vent, not from anything that I transmitted (adrenaline or body language). I eventually asked other dog handlers if they had ever seen this behavior and four other handlers shared that their dogs showed similar scenting behavior while traveling in cars.

Rachel also loved it when I received mail or a package from my mother. She'd ignore all my other mail, but would wag her tail when she picked up on the scent left on the envelope or card from my mother. I believe that Rachel probably associated my mother with snacks because my mother always gave Rachel a yummy treat when I arrived at her home! This might explain why Rachel was always so excited when she discriminated my mother's scent from the scent of other people.

Selecting a Scent Article

When selecting a scent article to present to a MAR trailing dog, always look for an item that has *direct-deposit* scent. By direct deposit I mean an item that has been in direct contact with the animal; for example, the missing pet's food dish, collar, brush, scratching post or bedding. It is quite risky to simply scent a MAR dog on the ground where the missing pet was last seen. Even if the owner of a missing cat tells you that he saw his lost kitty running across the lawn in a particular spot, you can't be sure the cat's smell is what the trailing dog will scent. It's possible that twenty minutes prior, a female bitch in heat walked by and urinated at that same spot. If you simply point to the ground, cue your MAR dog to "Search!" and expect her to follow the scent of the cat, the trailing dog may scent the bitch, thus making your success in trailing the cat minimal. Before you track a scent trail, you should always present the trailing or dual-purpose dog with a scent article as outlined in Chapter 10. The key to training a MAR dog is clear communication between the handler and the dog. This includes communicating to your dog exactly what scent you want him to follow and interpreting from his body language whether or not he's on the scent.

Internal Scent Sources

There are also internal sources of scent. "Bad breath" is actually the result of bacteria acting upon cells from inside the mouth and cells exhaled from the lungs.[15] This type of scent is one of the sources of scent that is used when training water-search dogs. Water-search (body recovery) dogs are trained to detect the presence of a human underneath water and assist dive teams in the recovery of drowning victims. When training water-search dogs, divers are placed below the surface of the water. Although the wetsuit may prevent the escape of shed skin cells, the breathing apparatus allows shed lung cells to bubble up to the surface of the water where the dogs can clearly detect scent. When an actual drowning victim is below the surface of the water, the entire body is producing scent. While the victim is no longer breathing or generating new skin cells, his or her body has begun the process of decomposition, a new form of scent dispersal. When you understand the nature of scent and how it is dispersed, the fact that a dog can smell a body that is below the surface of the water is not so surprising.

Vehicle Scent

An interesting issue regarding scent is whether or not a dog can be trained to follow what is called *vehicle scent*. Vehicle scent is the residual scent particles from a person seated inside a vehicle that is dispersed and deposited along roadway surfaces and alongside roads.

Why should you believe that a dog could follow human scent deposited from a moving vehicle? First, cars are not airtight. If cars were airtight, they would float, not sink, when they land in water. If cars were airtight, you would not smell skunk spray even when the windows are rolled up. Water, smoke, skunk odor and other environmental odors, can penetrate the cab of your car through both the ventilation system and the seams of the car windows. If a window or sunroof is open while traveling, even more scent is allowed to escape from the vehicle.

Bloodhounds and other search dogs have, in fact, successfully worked vehicle trails on criminal and missing person cases. One of the more famous cases was in May 1993 when an Aurora, Colorado, Bloodhound named Yogi tracked the scent trail of an abducted child named Alie Berrelez. Yogi followed a scent trail for seven hours and tracked seven miles through the city, onto a highway, and into a remote area of the woods where Alie's body was recovered by searchers.[16]

Police Bloodhounds have been known to follow scent dispersed from a moving car.

A friend who is a Michigan police Bloodhound handler has worked many successful vehicle scent trails. In one particular case, a burglary suspect used a rock to break a window and grab cigarettes in a "smash and grab" theft from a grocery store. An alarm signaled police, but the suspect fled prior to their arrival. Because this agency understood the capabilities of a Bloodhound to discriminate scent and work scent evidence, the Bloodhound was immediately brought in and scented on the rock. He worked from the crime scene up several blocks and approached an occupied pick up truck that had been pulled over by a state trooper. The state trooper witnessed the driver run a red light and was issuing a traffic citation. The Bloodhound proceeded to run up to the truck, wiggle with excitement, and jumped up and placed his paw on the driver, indicating to the handler that the suspect in the truck was the source of the scent. Inside the cab next to the driver were unopened packages of cigarettes, the brand taken from the store. The suspect confessed to the burglary and was arrested.

From my personal study of lost-dog behavior, I have interviewed many dog owners whose dogs were lost in unfamiliar areas, but eventually worked their way back to the owner's home. Many of these cases involved dogs who "mysteriously" followed the same route that the owner had traveled in their vehicle. The only plausible explanation, besides a mystical belief that the dog used a sixth sense, was that the dog was able to follow the vehicle trail of scent that came out of the owner's vehicle.

Do Animals Produce Individual Scent?

If you now believe that dogs can smell people through water, follow the scent of a person who has left in a vehicle, detect the presence of cancer cells, and tell the difference between the scent of one person from another, then it will not be too difficult for you to believe that a dog can differentiate the scent of one cat from another cat or one dog from another dog. The idea behind this concept is that all animals have their own unique scent.

Take cats for example. The idea that one cat smells different from another cat may seem like a far-fetched idea to some people. But kittens with their eyes still closed have been known to hiss at the presence of a cat other than their mother just as puppies with their eyes still closed have been known to growl at the presence of the scent of a dog other than their mother. Many dog owners, especially show dog handlers, confirm that their dogs recognize the scent of one particular dog who was familiar to them in the midst (at a large dog show) of many look-alike dogs. Ranchers confirm that lambs in the midst of a pasture filled with ewes will successfully find their mothers, regardless of the fact that most of the ewes look similar.

Recent research on scent indicates that the components that make animal (as well as human) scent unique can be found in genes. According to science writer Kenneth Chiacchia, Ph.D., scientists have discovered that molecules known as "major histocompatibility complex" (MHC) proteins sit on the surface of all body cells and make up the body's "bar code system."[17] Every person, and potentially every animal, has a unique combination of six MHC genes. In the 1970s, immunologists began to study whether it was possible that every cell in the human body carries a molecular fingerprint and whether or not animals use this system to identify each other by smell.[18] According to Chiacchia, researchers successfully trained mice to identify the urine of other mice. They discovered that the mice could also successfully recognize each another by sniffing blood serum. They discovered what Chiacchia called "a bouquet of chemicals" that seemed to convey an individual scent.[19]

Researchers also speculated that MHC proteins pick up other available molecules of scent (shampoos, food, oils, etc.) to create an individual, unique scent.[20] The brand of dog food, treats, and shampoos used on a dog, combined with the unique genetic makeup of a particular dog appear to help craft a unique, individual scent, one that a properly trained dog can be taught to follow. Thus, both genetics (DNA) and environment (food, shampoos, etc.) appear to play an important role in creating a unique, individual scent. For further reading on scent, see the Resource section.

Chapter Footnotes

1. William G. Syrotuck, *Scent and the Scenting Dog* (Mechanicsburg, PA: Barkleigh Productions Inc., 2000), p. 30.

2. Angela Eaton Snovak, *Guide to Search-and-Rescue Dogs* (Hauppauge, New York: Baron's Educational Series, 2004), p. 41.

3. Syrotuck, op. cit, p. 30.

4. Ibid., p. 53.

5. Ibid., p. 53-56.

6. Ibid., p. 56.

7. Ibid., p. 63.

8. Bill Tolhurst, VSM, *The Silent Witness* (self published, 2000, ISBN 0-9667989-3-7), p. 86-88.

9. Catherine F. Brey and Lena F. Reed, *The Complete Bloodhound* (New York, NY: Howell Book House, 1980), p. 141.

10. Jeff Schettler granted me permission to reprint the cited (currently unpublished) text that he authored.

11. Syrotuck, op. cit, p. 19.

12. Ibid.

13. Leon Whitney D.V.M., *Dog Psychology: The Basis of Dog Training* (Howell, 1976), p. 34.

14. Rick Boling, "Can Dogs Sniff Out Cancer?" *Animals* (Sept/Oct 1996), p. 14-17.

15. Syrotuck, op. cit, p. 35.

16. The story of Yogi the bloodhound tracking Alie Berrelez can be found at www.alie.org/generic.html or at www.leba98.com.

17. Kenneth B. Chiacchia, "Who Goes There? The Body's System for Generating Individual Scent," *Advanced Rescue Technology* (June/July 2004): p. 46.

18. Ibid.

19. Ibid, p. 47.

20. Ibid, p. 48.

Chapter 6

HOW LOST PETS BEHAVE

Search-and-rescue professionals are trained extensively in the analysis of lost person behaviors. Individuals who want to succeed in finding lost pets must be trained in the equivalent analysis: lost pet behaviors. Knowing how lost pets behave (as well as the humans who lose them and the rescuers who find them) enables you to know how and where to search.

There is a *science* to finding lost people, and a lot of that knowledge can be applied to finding lost pets. Professionally trained searchers don't wander aimlessly in the woods when searching for a missing hiker. Instead, an organized search plan is implemented based on the knowledge of the behavioral patterns of lost people. For example, backpackers behave differently and travel different distances when lost than do berry pickers or hunters. Search and rescue managers are so familiar with these varying patterns of behavior that they can often predict where a lost person is most likely to be found. Backpackers rely on trails with a set destination in mind, but complications occur when trail conditions change. Berry pickers intend to stay in one area (to pick berries) and are typically unequipped and unprepared (no food or water) for being outdoors when they become lost. Hunters concentrating on following game more than navigation can easily become lost, often ending up deep within the woods.

What is known about the behavioral patterns of lost pets? Lost dogs tend to act differently than lost cats. That's because dogs are truly different animals! The methods that should be used to search for a lost dog, an outdoor-access cat who has vanished from his territory, and an indoor-only cat who has escaped his house are entirely different. For example, dogs tend to travel distances and are often picked up by rescuers who determine their fate. Outdoor-access cats may be prohibited or interrupted from coming home, and indoor-only cats who escape outdoors often panic and typically hide in silence near their escape point. Searchers must take into account these differences.

Additionally, the behavior of owners who lose their pets, as well as the behavior of individuals who find lost pets ("strays") impacts the chances of whether or not a lost pet will be returned home.

How Lost Cats Behave
Lost cats tend to be easier to find than lost dogs because they do not travel as far as dogs, and are less likely to be picked up by people who capture and keep them. Lost cat behavior varies according to where the cat has established his territory (outdoor or indoor), and also his temperament.

Outdoor Access Cats
Cats are territorial. When a cat who is allowed to go outdoors suddenly vanishes, it means that *something has happened* to that cat to interrupt his normal behavior of returning home. The disappearance could mean that the cat is injured, trapped, or deceased. Most owners don't realize that as a protective measure, cats who are sick, injured, or panicked will hide in silence, a behavior called the *silence factor*. A sudden disappearance could also mean that the cat was transported out of the area, either intentionally (by an irate neighbor who trapped the cat) or unintentionally (by the cat climbing into an open, parked van). It could even mean that the cat was displaced into unfamiliar territory, something as simple as being chased by a dog, which caused the cat to hide under a neighbor's deck one block away from home. When this happens, the temperament of the cat influences how he behaves. When displaced, some cats are so panicked and afraid that they will remain in hiding for weeks and never return home while others will break cover within hours and slink home.

Indoor Only Cats

The territory for an indoor-only cat is inside his home. When an indoor-only cat escapes outdoors, he is displaced into unfamiliar territory. Usually, the cat seeks the first place that offers concealment and protection. The instinct to hide in silence is a primary protection from predators. How long a cat remains in hiding and what he does next is dependant upon temperament. Baited humane traps are a highly effective method for recovering displaced, panicked cats who are hiding and are very hungry.

Baited humane traps are a highly effective method for recovering displaced, panicked cats.

Temperament and Distance

Temperament influences actions. How a cat behaves in his normal territory influences how he behaves when he becomes lost or displaced into unfamiliar territory. Cat owners must use a search strategy based on the specific behavior of their cat. There are four basic feline temperaments that influence how cats behave when lost.

Curious/clown cats. These are gregarious cats who get into trouble easily, run to the door to greet a stranger, and are not afraid of anything. When displaced, cats of this nature might initially hide, but then they will roam. The best initial strategy for recovery is to place florescent, lost-cat posters within a minimum five-block radius. Also, you should interview neighbors in a door-to-door search and thoroughly check possible hiding places in nearby yards and other areas within a close proximity to the escape point. Do *not* assume that the cat will meow or come when you call!

Gregarious cats who are not easily frightened are likely to travel when displaced.

Standoffish cats. Aloof cats don't seem to care much about people. When a stranger comes in the house, they stand back and watch. When displaced, a standoffish cat is initially likely to hide, but eventually comes to the door, meows, or possibly travels. The strategy for finding a cat of this temperament is to search nearby hiding places, interview neighbors door-to-door and search their yards. If these efforts do not produce results, consider setting a baited humane trap.

Cautious cats. These cats are generally stable, but show occasional shyness. They like people, but when a stranger comes to the door, they dart away and hide. Some cautious cats peek out, and eventually investigate. When displaced, they are likely to immediately hide in fear. If not scared off from a hiding place, the cautious cat typically returns to the point from which he escapes, or meows when the owner comes to look for him. This behavior is observed within the first two days (after the cat has gained confidence) or not until seven to ten days later when hunger or thirst has reached a peak. There is such a consistent pattern in cats that hide, but then respond after seven days, that it is called the *threshold* *phenomenon*. The strategy when searching for cautious cats is to conduct a tightly focused search in neighbors' yards and to set baited humane traps.

Catatonic/xenophobic cats. Xenophobia means "fear or hatred of things strange or foreign." Xenophobic cats are afraid of everything that is new or unfamiliar. Their fearful behavior is hardwired into their character; it is caused by genetics and/or kittenhood experiences (nature and/or nurture). These cats hide when a stranger comes into their home, and they typically will not come out until company has left. They do not do well with human contact (being held, petted, etc.) and they are easily disturbed by *any* change in the environment. When displaced, they bolt, then hide in silence. They tend to remain in the same hiding place and become almost catatonic, immobilized with fear. If observed by a person other than their owners, they are often mistaken as being untamed or feral. The primary strategy to recover these fearful cats is to set baited humane traps. Xenophobic cats who are lost (and never recovered) are routinely absorbed into the feral cat population.

How Lost Dogs Behave

Dogs are much more difficult to recover than lost cats because they travel farther, and they are more likely to be picked up by rescuers who then determine their fate. There are two major factors that influence the distances that lost dogs travel: temperament and circumstances. Relevant circumstances include weather, terrain, appearance, and population density.

Temperament

How a dog behaves toward strangers influences how far she will travel (when lost) before someone intervenes and rescues her. Lost dogs are classified in three primary behavioral categories: gregarious, aloof and xenophobic.

Gregarious dogs. Wiggly-butt, friendly dogs are inclined to go directly to the first person who calls them. Depending on the terrain and population density where the dog is lost, these dogs are generally found close to home or picked up by someone close to the escape point. Gregarious dogs are often "self-adopted" by individuals (outside of shelters and rescue groups) who find and keep them rather than taking them to a shelter.

Gregarious, friendly dogs who approach strangers easily are often picked up and "rescued" close to their escape point.

Aloof dogs. Dogs with aloof temperaments are wary of strangers and will initially avoid human contact. Eventually, they might be willing to approach people once they have overcome fear and are hungry enough. While these dogs can travel a great distance, aloof dogs eventually can be enticed with food and patience, typically by experienced rescuers who know how to approach and capture a wary dog. These dogs are often recovered by rescue-group volunteers. However, their wariness can be easily misinterpreted as the result of abuse. In addition, these dogs are often not recovered for weeks or months after escape, giving them the physical appearance (skinny, dirty, poor haircoat, etc.) of a homeless, abused, and unloved dog.

Xenophobic dogs. Dogs with xenophobic temperaments (due to genetics and/or puppyhood experiences or both) are more inclined to travel farther and are at a higher risk of being hit by cars. Due to their cowering, fearful behavior, people assume these dogs were abused, and even if the dog has identification tags, often refuse to contact the previous owner because they think the owner was abusive. Some of these panic-stricken dogs even run from their owners! It may be necessary to use a "magnet dog" to get close enough to capture a fearful dog or to use baited humane traps.

Circumstances Surrounding the Disappearance

The circumstances under which a dog becomes lost can have a significant impact on her behavior. A dog who digs out from a yard to explore a scent is likely to travel a short distance before she is found, meandering and doubling back as she explores a scent. On the other hand, a dog who bolts in panic due to fireworks or thunder will take off at a blind run and can run for several miles.

Weather. A dog who escapes on a beautiful spring day may travel farther than one who escapes during a snowstorm. Extreme weather conditions (snow, hail, rain, sweltering heat) will decrease the distances that lost dogs travel because they are likely to seek shelter and stay in one place.

Terrain. A dog who escapes in a residential area will not travel as far as a dog who escapes in a mountainous area. Fences that create barriers will influence a dog's travel since she tends to take the path of least resistance while traveling. Cactus, heavy brush, and steep cliffs can influence whether or not a dog will continue on a certain path or change directions.

People are more inclined to rescue small dogs because they look vulnerable and are easier to transport and house than large dogs.

Appearance. What a dog looks like can influence how quickly she is picked up by a rescuer. In general, most people are more likely to grab a friendly looking Labrador Retriever and less inclined to grab a Pit Bull that they perceive as aggressive. Also, size matters. People are more inclined to pick up small dogs because they look vulnerable and are easier to transport and house than large dogs. In addition, people are more likely to attempt to rescue a purebred dog who they perceive to have more value than a mixed breed dog. When the average motorist sees a mixed breed dog trotting down the sidewalk, his impression is often that the dog belongs in the neighborhood or that she is a homeless stray. When that same person sees a Boston Terrier or an Old English Sheepdog, he is inclined to believe that the dog must be lost because she is a "valuable purebred dog."

Population density. A dog who escapes in Manhattan will travel a shorter distance than a dog who escapes in the Rocky Mountains or in rural farmland. When dogs escape into areas with a high number of people, their chances of being found close to the escape point are increased. But in areas with an extremely low number of people, they tend to travel farther and their chances of being found close to the escape point are decreased. A dog who escapes in the middle of the night will travel farther before being seen than a dog who escapes during the daytime.

Owner Behaviors

Owners often behave in ways that inhibit the chance of recovering a lost pet. Some owners have a "wait and see" approach, believing the pet will return home (like Lassie did). By the time they start actively looking for the dog, the vital first few hours are gone. Other owners have "tunnel vision" and fail to find their dog or cat because they focus on wrong theories. They may assume the dog was "stolen and sold to research" when in fact the dog might have been rescued and put up for adoption through a local rescue group. Some owners experience "grief avoidance" and quickly give up the search effort because they really believe they will never see their pet again. They feel helpless and alone, often discouraged by others who rebuke them and tell them, "It was just a dog," or "You'll never find your cat."

The level of human-animal bond influences the recovery efforts. People with a strong bond to their pets go to extremes to find their lost dog or cat. They accomplish the daunting task of visiting all shelters, posting flyers, and contacting rescue groups while maintaining a full-time job and other family commitments.

A primary reason why so many lost cats are never found is that cat owners focus their entire search efforts on posting lost-cat flyers and searching the local shelter. Although these techniques are important and should not be overlooked, the primary technique to recover a missing cat is to obtain permission from all neighbors to enter their yards and conduct an aggressive, physical search for the missing cat, setting baited humane traps when necessary. Simply asking a neighbor to "look for" the lost cat is not sufficient. Neighbors are not going to crawl on their bellies under their decks or houses to search for someone else's cat! It is the responsibility of owners or professional pet detectives or pet rescuer volunteers to do this.

Rescuer Behavior

The behavior of people who find loose, stray dogs differs from the behavior of people who find stray cats. People who find stray dogs with skittish temperaments often misinterpret the dog's behavior. They assume that the cowering, fearful dog was abused, when the dog really has a fearful temperament and has been shy and afraid since puppyhood due to genetics and/or experiences. Dogs found in rural areas are often assumed to be dumped and homeless, simply based on location. Many rescuers never think a dog such as this is lost. Some people who find a stray dog without a collar automatically assume she is homeless and immediately work to place the dog, rather than attempt to find the dog's owner. In addition, the *first* place where the owner of a lost dog will search for their dog—the local shelter—is typically the *last* place that someone who finds a loose dog will take her due to the fear of euthanasia!

When people find stray cats, they also misinterpret behaviors. When rescuers observe a cat with a fearful temperament they assume, based on skittish behavior, that the cat is a feral. While it is true that feral, untamed cats who are unaccustomed to human contact will hiss, spit, twirl, lunge, and urinate when humanely trapped, this "wild animal" behavior is also common in cats who have xenophobic temperaments. (We've learned this at Missing Pet Partnership because for the past ten years we've talked to owners who had fearful cats that had to be humanely trapped in order to be recovered. The owners of these kitties have verified that their cats exhibited wild behavior while in the humane trap. These behaviors are a reflection of a fearful *temperament*, not a lack of *tameness*.) Shelter and trap-neuter-return (TNR) workers should scan all feral cats for microchips and conduct research by checking classifieds ads and lost-cat reports to determine if the new "feral" who shows up in the colony or shelter is actually someone's xenophobic pet cat who escaped outdoors, perhaps several weeks or months before.

Chapter 7
THE SCIENCE OF SEARCHING

Bomb-dog handlers never work a trained bomb dog without first learning everything there is to know about how explosives are packaged, where they are most likely to be placed, and the most effective and safe methods to detect them. In the same manner, a dog who is trained to find lost pets is worthless if you don't know anything about *how* and *where* to search for lost pets. In this chapter you will learn *how* to search by examining the three primary search techniques:

- *Hasty search*, which is a rapid search of high probability search areas
- *Efficient area search*, which is a systematic, detailed search of high probability search areas
- *Thorough area search*, which is a slow, meticulous search of all areas

Following this discussion on *how* to search is a discussion on *where* to search for lost pets.

Hasty Search
A hasty search is a rapid search of high probability search areas and is designed to locate a lost pet quickly. In traditional search-and-rescue, it is a technique used during the initial hours of a search operation. For example, a case in which a hiker is lost in the woods, trained searchers

are sent out immediately to walk the major trail systems leading away from the point where the hiker was last seen. The searchers walk at a fairly brisk pace, calling the lost person's name in the hopes he would be found alive, close to the trail system. In the case of a missing fisherman, searchers would immediately walk the banks of the river near the point last seen, walking at a brisk pace and calling for the lost fisherman in the hopes he is still alive and near the river. Meanwhile, the search manager would be at base camp developing a detailed plan, including mapping out segmented areas where searchers would next be sent to conduct a detailed "efficient" area search (of the woods or river).

A popular hasty search technique used in both SAR and in MAR work is to use a trailing dog to establish a direction of travel. The use of a trailing dog in this case is considered a hasty search because it is typically conducted early on in the search effort, and it does not require strategy or planning. The trailing-dog handler presents a scent article that contains scent of the missing person or animal at the point last seen and follows his dog as she follows the trail of scent.

When I worked as a police officer searching for lost people, I was typically called during the first hours of the search operation to conduct a hasty search with my Bloodhound, A.J. In many cases, I worked A.J. on the scent trail during the same time the search manager was calling up the larger group of ground searchers, many of whom would not be deployed into the segmented search area for hours. That's because it takes time to set up a command post, develop a search plan, segment areas on the map, and write up individual assignments for the area search teams. On several occasions A.J. found the missing person, or enabled searchers ahead of us to find the person, eliminating the need for additional searchers.

The advantage of conducting a hasty search is that you have a good chance of finding the missing person or pet by getting into the search area quickly. A hasty search is what is conducted when a dog owner first discovers that his dog is missing. Typically, the dog owner will immediately walk, run or drive through the neighborhood to search for the dog who escaped from the yard. This is a successful technique in recovering a lost dog, but it has drawbacks. The disadvantage of conducting a hasty search is that you sacrifice witness development in exchange for the potential of catching up with the dog. When a dog owner is busy rushing down the street calling the lost dog, he will likely miss speaking with the neighbor who might tell them she saw the dog trotting in the opposite direction just twenty minutes prior.

In MAR work, hasty searches are used for species that are able to travel fast and far. Animals such as dogs, horses, and livestock who have the ability to travel a great distance in a short amount of time are candidates for hasty searches. However, animals such as cats, snakes, hamsters, or lizards, who travel short distances require a very different search technique, an efficient and/or thorough search.

Efficient Area Search

An efficient area search is a systematic, detailed search of high probability search areas that are likely to be productive in finding the lost person or pet. In traditional SAR work, this is the technique in which ground teams are each given assignments to search a specific area. They are usually given a map (topographical, if the search is in the wilderness) with a clearly defined area that includes boundaries. The team is expected to search their assigned area for the missing person by looking, listening and, if they have an area search dog, by watching the search dog for an alert (e.g., sniffing, quick change of direction, tail wagging) that the dog has detected human scent.

Both cat-detection dogs and dual-purpose dogs are used in MAR work to conduct efficient area searches. Having obtained permission to enter neighbors' yards, the MAR technician directs her dog to sniff around every conceivable hiding place, including decks, porches, wood piles, piles of trash, sheds, and underneath houses. I've personally performed many efficient area searches in which I would have passed over physical evidence (tufts of cat fur, bone chips, and blood from where a coyote killed a cat) if my search dog had not alerted.

Before any search work begins, the MAR technician interviews the pet owner and asks about the missing pet's specific behavior in order to develop a "profile" of the lost pet. While developing the profile, the MAR technician also considers the geographical features and terrain of the area to be covered (open farmland, residential or wooded); environmental factors (summer in Arizona vs. winter in Illinois); and the typical lost pet behavior of that particular species of animal. These three factors—terrain, environment, and behavior—determine the size of the area that initially needs to be searched.

Besides the obvious goal of attempting to physically locate the lost pet, a secondary goal when conducting an efficient area search is to tell the pet owner whether or not their missing pet is located within the search area. This is critical because discovering that a lost pet is *not* within the high probability search areas enables the pet owner to begin to expand the search area. (In Chapter 14 you can read a case study of how discovering that a missing cat named Tony was no longer in his neighborhood actually helped his owner find him.)

Detection equipment, such as an amplified listening device, can be used when conducting efficient area searches for cats.

Efficient area searches are used for species that aren't initially likely to travel far. While a cat certainly has the ability to travel several miles, cats are more inclined to hide, a few blocks away from home, or become trapped, than they are to travel several miles. Cats who are sick, injured, or panicked are likely to hide in silence within their territory or near their escape point. Several factors influence the distance and rate of travel, but for the most part, the initial search for a lost cat should be an efficient search beginning at the cat owner's residence or the point last seen.

Unlike a hasty search, an efficient search involves a concerted effort to contact neighbors and potential witnesses to determine if anyone has seen, heard, or smelled anything unusual. Neighbors who catch a glimpse of a cat matching the description of the lost cat can help narrow the search area and increase the probability of recovery. However, witnesses can be unreliable and many false sightings are possible, especially in cases of generic-looking cats (e.g., black cats). MAR technicians can utilize detection equipment, such as an amplified listening device, search camera, or night vision equipment, when conducting efficient searches. MAR technicians are trained to look for physical evidence—tufts of fur, tracks, bloodstains, ground disturbances, or flies—while looking in every conceivable hiding place. These are clues that might be overlooked in a hasty search and can lead to the discovery of the animal.

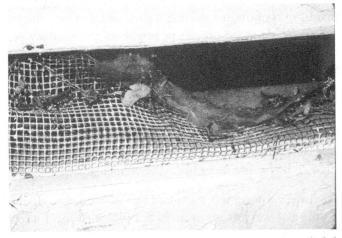

Clumps of cat hair clinging to wire mesh proved to be high probability evidence in the search for Manual. He was eventually found trapped under a neighbor's house in a similar kind of location.

On several lost-cat cases, I've located what I call "high probability" evidence: physical evidence that identifies a particular area as being a high probability search area. The most common form of high probability evidence is the accumulation of cat hair fibers deposited by outdoor-access cats. These clumps of hair are created by the repetitive movement of a cat rubbing against a stationary item when the cat moves in and out of his territory. In one case, I found an accumulation of cat hair fibers on mesh wire. Manual, a fourteen-year-old cat, had been missing for a month.

The high probability evidence indicated that Manual spent much of his time under his own house. In spite of a thorough search under his home, I did not find him there. Instead, Manual was found trapped under a neighbor's house directly behind his own home. The neighbor had placed new screens at the basement access points of the home, entombing Manual under the house. In spite of being trapped for several weeks without food and only occasional rainwater, Manual survived!

An efficient search should actually be used in searches for all species, even for animals likely to travel long distances, such as dogs and horses. An efficient search is conducted as a follow up to a hasty search in these cases, especially if there is no obvious exit point (from the yard) and there is no witness to the escape. The owner may immediately suspect theft. However, a detailed search of the yard should be conducted (checking for loose boards) to confirm that the dog is gone and that he is not trapped, injured, or deceased in the owner's or neighbors' yards. Many pet owners have launched massive, wide-ranging hasty searches for missing dogs and horses only to eventually discover that the animal was very close to home.

I know of cases in which a missing horse fell down an abandoned well on the owner's own property, a dog was trapped for three days in a gazebo in his own back yard, and a dog was entangled in cable wire for two days under his own home, but never barked or whined.

In another case, a woman was convinced that someone had climbed into her yard (the gate was locked) to steal her Bulldog. When I interviewed her about potential exit points through the fence, she acknowledged that her dog could have squeezed under the fence into her neighbor's yard. I asked her if she had searched her neighbor's yard and she said she had looked over the fence and called her dog, but he had not responded. In her mind, he was not there. I instructed her to *search* her neighbor's yard. An hour later, her brother called and told me the woman had found her dog—he drowned in the neighbor's pool. In all of these cases, the owners launched massive search efforts, yet they could have located their missing pet quicker if they had followed a hasty search with an efficient area search.

Thorough Area Search

A thorough area search is a slow, meticulous search of an area, and is used for animals, such as hamsters, lizards, turtles and snakes, who are not likely to travel very far. In law enforcement, a thorough area search is conducted when searching for physical evidence, such as a shell casing used in a homicide that landed in tall grass. The search technique for this type of evidence involves a slow, methodical, and intense search of a small area.

The goal of a thorough area search is to search every square inch of a small area to see if the animal can be located. In many cases, the search for a missing cat will start out as an efficient search, but will involve portions in which a thorough search is conducted. For example, a MAR technician might conduct an efficient search moving from yard to yard in a neighborhood until her MAR dog suddenly alerts to a wood pile. At that point, the technician begins a meticulous, thorough search by moving the wood, piece by piece, as she attempts to determine if the missing cat is trapped, hiding or deceased inside the pile.

The author and her search dog, Rachel, conduct a thorough search for a lost box turtle suspected of burrowing into juniper bushes.

Search Probability Theory

To learn *where* to search for lost pets, you need to understand the principles of search probability theory.

Search probability theory is a branch of mathematics used in traditional search-and-rescue to estimate the likelihood that a missing person is within a particular area; it can be applied to finding lost pets, as well. *There is a higher probability of success if you focus search efforts and deploy resources in the areas where the lost person or animal is most likely to be found.* Typically, a map is divided into segmented areas that are assigned numbers that prioritize which areas should be searched first. This prioritization is based on the terrain, knowledge of lost person/animal behaviors, and information gathered about that particular missing person/animal.

Traditional SAR teams searching for a missing person have the advantage of working with a large volunteer base, often over the span of several days. But as a MAR technician, you are likely to work alone or with a limited number of resources. Unless you have a large team of searchers, several search dogs, and several days to conduct a search operation, you can never effectively search an entire possible search area. Fortunately, in the case of lost cats, the majority are found within a two-block radius of their home. Even though there are cases in which a lost cat travels farther, a detailed area search within a one- to two-block proximity of the point last seen increases the probability of a successful recovery.

Search probability theory means that you should focus efforts in combing the *probable* search areas where a missing dog, cat, or other species is most likely to be found.

Establishing Direction

One key to narrowing a search area is to establish the most likely direction of travel. A lost dog who could conceivably travel five miles in any direction creates a search radius of seventy-eight square miles (*see Diagram 6, page 80*). One method used to discover which direction the lost dog went is to obtain witness statements by going door to door, asking neighbors if they have seen the lost dog. This can produce information, including the dog's direction of travel as well as a timeline of when she initially left the neighborhood.

A well-trained MAR trailing dog can also be used to establish the direction of travel. However, a poorly trained dog can lead the search in the wrong direction. This is why it is critical for all MAR dogs to be properly trained and proven through certification.

Either of these techniques, witness statements or a MAR trailing dog who establishes a direction of travel, can enable a pet owner to focus his attention more effectively. Posting florescent "Reward for Lost Dog" posters along the path the lost dog traveled increases the probability that someone who saw the dog, someone who has the dog, or someone who knows who has the dog will see the posters and call the owner.

Place florescent posters along the confirmed travel path of the lost dog to increase the probability of finding the lost dog.

Establishing the direction of travel can dramatically reduce the possible search area from seventy-eight square miles down to a manageable six square miles. (You can read examples of how MAR trailing dogs successfully established a direction of travel and helped recover lost dogs in Chapter 14).

The Dog Handler as Investigator

Professional searchers within traditional SAR are taught that they are not searching for a missing person. Instead, they are searching for clues and physical evidence that can lead to the discovery of the person. In MAR work, instead of looking only for a live pet, you must search also for clues, witnesses, physical evidence, and information. This requires that you do not think only in terms of working as a dog handler, but that you also develop the mindset of an *investigator*.

Diagram 6

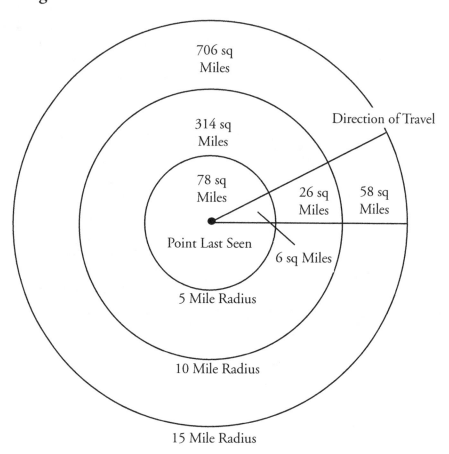

706 sq Miles

314 sq Miles

78 sq Miles

Direction of Travel

26 sq Miles

58 sq Miles

Point Last Seen

6 sq Miles

5 Mile Radius

10 Mile Radius

15 Mile Radius

A confirmed direction of travel is critical in recovering a lost dog. A five mile radius has a search area of 78 square miles. But, by establishing a direction of travel (with a trailing dog or witness statements) the search area can be reduced to just 6 square miles.

As an investigator, never rely strictly on the MAR search dog when tracking a lost pet. This is a guiding principle in law enforcement and SAR work, as well. As good and as helpful as they are, search dogs are never treated as the only answer to solving all cases. That's because a search dog's work is never 100-percent accurate, and many variables can interfere with scent work, including the handler's misinterpretation of what his dog indicates. I know this first-hand because I learned a valuable lesson through a major mistake early in my pet detective career.

In 1998, I responded with my search dog, Rachel, to track a Poodle who had been missing for two days. The missing dog was known to be a fence jumper and would often end up a quarter-mile from his home at a community park. I responded to his residence, collected scent material, and presented the scent of the Poodle to Rachel in front of the home. Although the backyard was five acres of steep terrain and covered with thick brambles and vegetation, I never bothered to search that area because I believed what the owner suspected: the Poodle had left the area. I also fully trusted that Rachel could follow the scent trail. Rachel did pick up a scent trail and led me down to the community park where we spoke to a witness who claimed he saw the dog there the same day he vanished. I drove home, excited that Rachel had worked yet another successful case. Wrong! The owners of the Poodle called me two days later to tell me they had found their dog; birds of prey circling above their property helped pinpoint his body. The Poodle apparently attempted to jump over the back fence, but caught his collar on the fence and strangled to death.

As it turns out, Rachel actually did a great job in her trailing work on this case. I learned that the Poodle had traveled from his home to that community park the day *before* he disappeared (the witness had his days confused), and this explained why Rachel trailed to the park. The Poodle case taught me two critical lessons about searching for lost pets: 1) an entire investigation *should not* revolve around the work of my search dogs; and 2) all hasty searches with a trailing dog should be followed up with an efficient area search.

Whether the search is for a missing Greyhound (a dog who could potentially travel many miles) or a displaced cat (a cat who is likely hiding near the escape point), a detailed efficient area search must be conducted for all lost animals to make certain they are not still in the area and concealed from view. After the Poodle case, I stopped focusing on only using trailing dogs to find lost pets. Instead, I worked to develop an entire *system* of finding lost pets, one that mirrored the same search management principles and methods that are used in law enforcement to find criminals, missing people, and physical evidence.

I met with a pet detective (no longer in business) in 2001 who was preparing to launch a pet detective company. This was a business meeting (between a veterinarian, myself, and this particular pet detective) to explore different options for the emerging pet detective industry. The pet detective had a business that had been in existence for nine months in which he had responded with his tracking dog on many lost-pet searches.

When the veterinarian asked him just how many lost pets this particular dog had helped locate, the pet detective said, "None, actually. By the time I'm called out, the scent trail is too old. I see the dogs as more of a marketing tool that will draw customers in." MAR dogs should be properly trained and used as an *investigative* tool, not as a "marketing tool" used to capture clients or generate business revenue!

Your canine partner is there to aid *you* in the effort to locate a lost pet. Although many pet owners believe that a MAR dog is *the* answer to finding their lost pet, the reality is that your dog will be successful in locating lost pets only for a portion of your investigations. There are many cases where a search dog will be ineffective, but a combination of properly placed lost-dog posters, a baited humane trap, an amplified listening device, a three million candlepower spotlight, or a search of lost-pet web sites will be what actually brings a lost pet home. Your role as a dog handler should be to take the time and effort required to properly train a dog until she is proficient in finding lost pets, move toward having your dog certified through testing, and to then utilize that dog to the best of your abilities in an ethical manner.

Chapter 8
MAR TRAINING FUNDAMENTALS

Training time for a MAR dog varies. Depending on the drive level of the dog, what discipline you plan to train, and the time you are able to invest, it may take four months to more than eighteen months to train a dog to certification level. That estimate factors in training five days a week.

Training any search dog is a *process* that should not be rushed. As tempting as it is to get out there and search for lost pets, you are doing a disservice to yourself, the dog, your community, and the emerging pet detective industry if you deploy your dog too quickly and work searches before the dog is ready.

There are a number of training fundamentals and concepts covered in this chapter that apply to all three MAR disciplines. You should familiarize yourself with these before training a dog specifically for MAR cat-detection, MAR trailing, or MAR dual-purpose work.

Frequency of Training

As with any training, you do not want to bore or burn out the dog. You are better off training several short sessions than you are teaching one long session; ten to fifteen minutes of work five days a week is more effective than an hour-long lesson once a week. You should work on the training techniques described in this book before feeding the dog so food rewards are more effective. For example, once a dog has learned the cue, "Push," you could require him to push on your leg before you give him dinner.

Moving Forward

The training methods in this book are a step-by-step format. I recommend that you follow these steps in the order outlined, with some variation depending on your individual needs (weather, terrain, etc.) and the dog.

Although I've suggested how much time to devote to each step, the dog will be the best indicator of when he's ready to move forward. When the dog consistently performs a step with precision, advance forward. If you attempt a new step and the dog makes a mistake or seems confused, back up to the previous step and work on that for a week before you attempt to move forward.

Rewards

An important reward for your dog is playing or interacting with the pet he is searching for. However, treats as supplementary rewards are also important. While you should be working with dogs who have a stronger love for playing with other dogs or cats than a love for treats, some dogs respond well to receiving a yummy after they've made a find. Other dogs are driven to play with toys, and these can be used as a supplemental reward. Allow the MAR dog to interact with the cat in the crate or the hidden dog he has found. Then, call the dog to you so his focus is back on you, and give him a treat or toy. I do not suggest using a clicker or giving food or toy rewards while a MAR trailing dog is in the midst of tracking a scent trail. My experience shows that verbal praise and encouragement are effective enough, and that clicking or giving treats while working a scent trail is too much of a distraction for most dogs. The dog must lock onto a scent trail and learn that his reward, playing with the cat/dog followed by treat or toy, comes at the end of the trail when he makes a find.

Cat-detection dog, Susie, prefers to play with target cat, Cheeto, before receiving a hot dog treat.

Vary Locations

Be sure to vary the locations where you train, starting out in areas with few distractions. While training MAR cat-detection dogs, you want to hide the cats in a variety of places, such as bushes, shopping centers, or under the deck of a house that belongs to family or friends. The same concept applies with MAR trailing dogs. Start in areas with few distractions, then set up more complex scent trails that begin and end in different settings (commercial areas, residential neighborhood, busy intersections, rural countryside, wooded wilderness, and grassy parks). Be sure the trailing dog and dual-purpose dog work scent trails on pavement, sand, asphalt, and grass. The dog must learn to ignore distractions, such as barking dogs, stray cats, construction noise, ocean waves, and other sights and sounds. Whenever you prepare to set up a trail (especially in advanced training), think of something different and challenging that you can introduce to the dog.

Clicker Training

Before I review the role of clicker training with MAR dogs, I should stress that I simply don't have the space in this book (or the experience) to teach you everything you need to know about clicker training. There are, however, many books and training videos on the topic of clicker training and the training concept called "positive reinforcement." I strongly recommend that you refer to the Resource section for a recommended reading list on the subject. In the next three chapters, I note where clicker training can be utilized.

As a MAR dog trainer, you need to know that when you click a behavior you want to reinforce, you must follow up quickly with a treat or other reward that the dog values. Normally, the reward is a small, soft, yummy treat. Before moving on to specific behaviors, the clicker must signal to the dog that a treat will follow; this motivates the dog to "earn" clicks. You'll probably only need one or two five-minute sessions consisting of rapid clicking and treating before your dog knows that a click means a treat is coming.

Once your dog understands that "click means treat," you are ready to shape his behavior. Begin the training session with a minute of rapid clicks with treats. Then, stop and watch the dog. Do not move. Do not talk. Your dog is likely to try different behaviors, such as sitting or barking, in an attempt to make you click and give him a treat. If the dog will sit easily, click and treat just as he sits. By doing this, you teach the dog that he can make the clicker "click" by sitting. Your silence, lack of action and lack of click/treating when the dog is doing anything other than sitting is how your dog learns.

I recommend you begin each training session with thirty seconds of clicking and treating. Next, select a new behavior you want to reinforce such as stay. Stop and watch the dog, and click immediately if he remains still for several seconds. It is fascinating to watch a dog exhibit different behaviors in an attempt to make the clicker click.

Recommended MAR Cues

In the past, dogs were taught commands, words that told the dog what to do. But the word, "command," often implies the use of force as in, "Do this or I'll make you do it." The recent shift in the dog training community toward more positive training methods has created a similar shift in vocabulary. Many positive trainers now use the word "cue" rather than "command," and I've elected to do the same in this book.

A cue is simply a transfer of information rather than an implication to do it "or else." The well-trained dog will *choose* to offer the requested behavior because he has been positively reinforced for doing so, and he knows good stuff will happen if he does. This is especially appropriate in MAR dog training, since the relationship between dog and human must be a close cooperative partnership.

There are a number of basic cues you will use while training a MAR dog. While you don't necessarily have to use these exact words, these are the ones I recommend. Most important, use cues consistently. Cues will be discussed in greater detail in the following training chapters.

"**Are you ready? You wanna work?**" This is a preparation cue for all MAR dogs. It is used to excite and "pump up" the dog right before he is released to start searching.

"**Kitty-kitty-kitty.**" This cue is used to teach a cat-detection or dual-purpose dog to associate the scent of cats with the word "kitty."

"**Find the kitty. Where's the kitty?**" During both training and on actual searches, this cue is used to encourage a cat-detection or dual-purpose search dog to continue searching for a lost cat.

"**Search!**" Use this cue right as you release the collar of a cat-detection, trailing dog, or dual-purpose dog and he moves forward and puts his nose to work.

"**Where?**" This is an encouragement cue for when a MAR dog has picked up the scent pool of the animal she is searching for. During training, you use this cue right as the dog picks up the airborne scent of a hidden pet. During an actual search, you use this cue when your dog gives an alert, a visible indication that she has detected the scent she is looking for. The "Where?" cue is used to encourage the dog to continue looking for the source of the scent (e.g., a cat or a decomposing body) that she's detected and to then pinpoint its exact location.

"**Check this!**" This cue is used only for cat-detection and dual-purpose dogs. It is used while conducting an area search when the handler directs where he wants his dog to sniff.

"**Push.**" All MAR dogs learn to signal their handler by scratching with a paw when an animal is inaccessible (e.g., behind a door, inside a shed, behind the screen of a crawl space under a house, etc.).

"**Dig-dig.**" This cue is used to teach all MAR search dogs to dig with both paws at animal decomposition scent.

"**This way.**" This is used for cat-detection and dual-purpose dogs to direct them to move in a new direction.

"**Take scent.**" This is used only for trailing dogs and dual-purpose dogs. You say, "Take scent," right as the dog sniffs the scent article.

"**Which way?**" This cue is used only for trailing and dual-purpose dogs. During trailing work, the dog who tracks a scent trail may stop and turn around when he has lost the scent trail. "Which way?" helps to confirm he is still on the trail, both in training and on actual searches.

"**Na-poo**" or "**Comp.**" Either of these decomposition cues can be used for all MAR dogs during training and actual searches. In many cases, there is a pet owner at your side as you work the MAR dog. For this reason, you should select a decomposition cue that does not clue the pet owner that you're asking the dog to detect the scent of death. "Na-poo" is an Indian word for "the dead" and is used by many forensic (cadaver) dog trainers to disguise the fact that the dog is searching for a body. "Comp" (short for decomposition) is another word used to disguise the fact the dog is searching for decomposition.

Dogs learn to associate one of these cues with animal decomposition scent because all MAR search dogs are trained to signal that they have detected the scent by scratching or digging at the source of this scent. You can use any word that you want to teach this cue, but cues such as, "Flat cat" or "Bones" should probably be avoided!

"**Leave it! Get to work!**" This cue is used for all MAR search dogs when they become distracted by the wrong scent during training and while working searches.

Cues for All Types of MAR Dogs

Search

All MAR dogs must be taught the "Search" cue. This is the starting point of every search that corresponds with the action of releasing the dog's collar. At first, you aren't training the dog to actually search for a cat or a dog, you are simply teaching him that it is rewarding for him to use his nose to search for a treat or a toy. It is a fun game that you can play often with your dog, even indoors if the weather does not permit working outside. Follow these simple steps:

1. Find an area with few distractions.

2. Start by playing with the dog and give the treat or toy for a moment to get him excited. Then grasp him by the collar. Toss the toy or treat a short distance in front of the dog.

3. Tease the dog by using the cue, "Are you ready? You wanna work?" Make eye contact with the dog if possible, and only say this cue twice. This is a tease cue you will use later just prior to sending the dog out to search.

Toss the dog's favorite treat or toy a short distance while restraining him.

4. At the precise moment that you release the dog by letting go of his collar so he can retrieve the toy or eat the treat, say the cue, "Search!" in an upbeat, excited voice.

5. Praise the dog when he/she reaches the toy or treat. His real reward, of course, is to play with you and the toy, or eat the treat, but verbal praise should be included in the reward process. If you are using a clicker to train, click right as he grabs the toy or eats the treat; then give him a second treat by hand. Follow up with verbal praise.

6. Continue playing this game, going through the above process no more than five times per session, twice a day, to avoid burn out. When the dog is doing well, begin throwing the treat or toy behind something (e.g., a couch, bushes, into tall grass, behind a car, etc.) so that the dog can't see where it landed (make sure it is findable, though). Send the dog off to "Search!" He should now be searching and using his nose. If you see the dog pick up the scent and sniff around, trying to pinpoint the source of the scent, use the cue, "Wherree? Wheerrreee?" This is a drawn out, upbeat, encouragement cue that is used during training when the dog is inside the scent cone. Eventually, "Wherree?" is used when you want the dog to pinpoint the source of a scent. Play these easy search games for at least one week before you move to the next step.

7. Next, you'll add a component that prepares the dog for another step. Holding the dog by the collar, toss the toy or treat, and then after the item lands, place your hand over the dog's eyes for a brief moment before you release him. This prepares the dog for when he isn't able to see where the toy is tossed. Cover his eyes as you give the "Are you ready? You wanna work?" cue, then remove your hand, release his collar and let him go right as you give the "Search" cue. Stay at this step for at least one week before you advance to the next step.

8. The next step is to cover the dog's eyes right as you toss the item. Take the same hand in which you held and tossed the toy or treat, and immediately reach over and cover the dog's eyes so he does not see where the item lands. You can still use the cue, "Are you ready? You wanna work?" even though you've already thrown the item.

The dog should understand the search game by now and is totally dependent on his nose to find the treat or toy.

Covering the dog's eyes after tossing a toy teaches him to rely on his nose and not his eyes when searching.

9. Once the dog understands the game and finds the object after you've covered his eyes, advance to hiding the object without throwing it. Secure the dog so he can watch you: tie him up, place him in a crate, or have a friend hold him. Walk around the area where he can still see you, touching various items with your hands to disperse your scent. In one of the places that you touch, place his treat or toy. Then put him though the search routine:

   "Are you ready? You wanna work?"

   "Ready?" (cover his eyes)

   "Search!" (release his collar)

10. The final phase of this training is to have the dog go out and search for a hidden object that he did not see you place. Secure the dog in a crate or around a corner, or have someone hold him out of view so that he does not see you hiding the treat or toy. You want to disperse your scent in the area by touching various objects and hiding the toy or treat in one of those places. Then place the dog in a sit, cover his eyes with your hand (this is now a cue that he is going to search), and use the three cues listed above. The dog should go out,

use his nose to find what you've hidden, and receive his reward. If he doesn't search with enthusiasm or seems confused, take a few steps back until he learns how to play the game.

Push and Dig-Dig

The "Push" and "Dig-dig" cues are used to train a dog to utilize his paw(s) to communicate information to you. There are two circumstances during a search in which a MAR dog might use his paws.

1. "Push" is used to get the dog to indicate the exact location where he has detected animal scent (e.g., door jam to a shed, screen at base of house, entrance to pipe, down a well) by pawing at it.

2. "Dig-dig" is used to get the dog to scratch with both paws to indicate the presence of animal decomposition scent.

Using a hammer and nail, poke holes in a baby jar lid to allow scent to escape from the jar. Fill the baby jar with treats that have a strong scent, such as hot dogs. Present the jar to the dog. Right as he sniffs the jar, click and treat (give treats that you have in a bait bag or pouch, not what's inside the baby jar). Don't worry about giving the "Push" cue just yet. You will add that later when he consistently paws at the jar. Move the jar away, then back in front of the dog, and click and treat right when the dog sniffs the jar. Repeat this process six to eight times per session for three days. On the fourth day, put the jar down on the ground a few feet in front of your dog. Click and treat only when his paw touches the jar. Initially, you may need to pick up the jar and touch his paw to the jar. Keep working at touching his foot to the jar, then wait for him to move his foot and touch the jar himself, even accidentally.

Once the dog realizes that you will click and treat when she touches the jar with her paw, *then* add the cue, "Push," right as she touches the jar and you click. Click and treat, praise and use the cue every time the dog touches the jar with her paw. Eventually, after the dog has learned to associate the cue, "Push," with pawing the jar, you can give the cue and wait for her to touch the jar. Immediately click and treat when she touches it.

The "Dig-dig" cue is used to teach the dog to use both paws to scratch (dig) at decomposition scent on the ground. Eventually, you'll use this cue to teach the dog to dig at the presence of animal decomposition scent

Place the jar on the ground in front of the dog, and click and treat when his paw touches it.

in dirt or on asphalt (see Chapter 12). For now, focus on teaching the cue by using treats or a buried toy. The training method used for this cue is similar to what you used to teach "Push."

Dig a small hole in soft dirt and place a baby food jar filled with hot dogs inside the hole. Do not cover the jar with dirt, just place it so the dog must paw at the jar to dislodge it. If the dog wants the jar badly enough, he will attempt to get at it by digging it out. Each time he touches the jar with his paw, you should click-treat-praise, and use the cue, "Dig-dig."

Place a jar filled with hot dogs in a hole in the ground.

The next step is to place the jar in the hole and cover it with dirt. Encourage and tease the dog to get the jar out. Right as he begins to dig, use the cue, "Dig-dig," to encourage him. If the dog becomes distracted by the click and treat, and he has trouble returning to the digging behavior (because he turns and fixates on the treats that you are holding), then don't use the clicker and a treat as the reward. Praise him verbally, and continue to repeat the "Dig-dig" cue as he's digging.

The next step is to teach the "Dig-dig" hand signal. I like to use a rapid waving motion with my fingers—a motion that simulates digging—as I keep my hand and wrist still. You can develop whatever hand signal you want as long as you are consistent in using it. Bury the jar, then encourage the dog to get the jar. Give the "Dig-dig" hand signal close to the jar as you give the "Dig-dig" verbal cue.

The next step is to teach the dog to "Dig-dig" at a scent on pavement. Smear a piece of hot dog on the pavement so the scent is there, but the hotdog is not. Point at the scent smear and tell the dog, "Check this." Praise him when he sniffs the spot, and then immediately give the "Dig-dig" cue with the hand signal. Immediately click-treat-praise when the dog digs at the hot dog scent. If the dog does not dig at the scent, go back and work on the buried jar with the hand signal before proceeding.

The final step is to use animal decomposition scent (instead of hot dog scent) along with the "Dig-dig" cue. (Refer to Chapter 12 for specifics on animal decomposition training.)

Reading a Dog

Regardless of how you want to train a MAR dog, you must be able to "read" the dog effectively. Reading a dog means that you learn to interpret his body language to determine whether or not he's picked up the target scent. For a trailing dog, you must interpret whether or not the dog is following the target scent, is off the target scent, or has diverted onto a different scent. For a cat-detection dog, you must interpret whether or not he has detected the scent of a live or deceased cat. While every dog is different, there are some general indications that most dogs will give. When a trailing dog stops moving forward and begins to focus, sniffing intently on a particular spot (a bush, a telephone pole, or a corner of a building), it is a good indication that he's diverted to animal urine (or feces). This is called "crittering."

Stopping to intently sniff on one particular spot can indicate that a search dog is distracted away from a scent trail.

Crittering can distract a dog and cause him to lose focus when following a scent trail. Anytime a dog diverts to the scent of another animal, you say, "Leave it," and offer resistance by anchoring the lead to break his focus from the critter's scent. Once the dog returns to work, praise him as you jog along to keep him focused on making a find. You can boost the dog's interest in the scent trail by offering verbal praise when he makes a correct turn and discouragement when he diverts to the scent of another animal.

My first three search dogs used different body language when they worked a scent. Rachel, the Weimaraner, worked off-lead within a fifteen-yard radius of where I walked. Because she was trained to work off-lead, I used hand signals and cues to direct where I wanted her to check. Rachel never left my sight unless she picked up the air scent of whatever she was looking for (person, firearm, cat, etc.). The only time she would take off from me was when she found the scent of what she was searching for. Just before she would take off, Rachel would jut her nose in the air (alert) as she sniffed the airborne scent. She also would elevate her stubby tail slightly above where she normally carried it. When I would see her nose lift and her tail elevate, I knew that she had picked up airborne scent of whatever we were looking for.

When Rachel found cadaver material, she would sniff rapidly and intensely, and would work quickly to pinpoint the decomposition odor. Her body would stiffen and she would not run or show enthusiasm like she did on live human scent. When she narrowed down the scent and pinpointed the decomposition material, Rachel would sniff it for a moment, elevate her tail lightly, squat, and pee. Rachel's urination was a consistent behavior at the presence of any human or animal decomposition (she also would scratch at it and sometimes drop and roll in the scent).

Rachel had specific body language when she came across the fresh scent of a live animal. When she came into the fresh scent pool of cat, her body would crouch into what I call a "creepy mode." As part of her bird dog instinct, she would dip her belly and body low to the ground as her tail wiggled rapidly. Once she pinpointed where the cat was, Rachel would freeze in place with her tail wiggling. It was such a pleasure to use her in pet searches because she had great enthusiasm when finding kitties!

When my Bloodhound, A.J., worked a scent trail, he moved at an ambling pace that resembled a camel's gait. A.J. never worked with his nose on the ground. Instead, he carried his head at the same level that any trotting dog would. If his nose ever dropped to the ground, it was because he was crittering. When he overshot a turn and lost the scent that he was trailing, he raised his head, shook his body, made eye contact with me and trotted back the way we came in his attempt to pick up the scent again. If he was not able to pick up a trail again, I usually presumed that the person or pet was picked up by a vehicle or that we had missed a turn.

When A.J. worked into the fresh scent pool of the person or pet he was looking for, he went into what I call a "butt wag." A.J.'s entire rear end would swing back and forth with obvious happiness. His tongue would loll from his mouth and his ear set would change, giving his face the distinct appearance that he was smiling! He would make direct eye contact with the particular person he was looking for, sit down in front of her and place his paw on her thigh.

Chase, also a Bloodhound, worked with her nose to the ground. She would look like the stereotypical Bloodhound, and was very photogenic. From the time she was a puppy, Chase loved to work close to the actual "track" where the person (or dog) walked. This was never anything that

I trained because I learned early on that it is not important where a dog places his nose, nor is it important how close to the track that the dog works. What is important is learning to read each of my dog's unique body language, and interpret whether or not they are following the scent I presented to them.

When Chase was on the scent, her nose would be on to the ground and she pulled hard into the harness. When she would overshot a turn, her head would come up, she would make direct eye contact with me, and she would shake off. But unlike A.J., Chase was not easy to read when she entered the scent pool of the person she was looking for. Her facial expression, primarily her ears, changed a bit, but she didn't get excited like A.J. or Rachel did when they made a find. Chase loved to roll in decomposition scent, but she didn't give the urination alert to mark dead scent like Rachel would. Thus, when I saw Chase sniff the ground and start to dip her shoulder as if to roll, I knew that she had made a decomposition find.

The point in sharing these examples is this: *Every dog is different.* You learn to read *your* dog by spending many hours, months and even years running behind him. Watch the dog in various scent situations. You can even learn by watching how the dog reacts to various scents around your home and yard. You'll notice that the dog will detect scents late in the evening and early in the cool morning that he didn't detect during the warm afternoon.

Learning to read a dog takes time. If you want to have a reliable trailing dog who you can trust, then spend time watching the dog and how he reacts to scent. In time, you will be able to accurately predict just what the dog will do when he encounters various scent conditions while working a scent trail.

Loose Dogs and Other Hazards

You will have to deal with, and prepare for, loose dogs and other hazards while working a MAR dog. When working a search, you run the risk of encountering loose dogs who may see you and your MAR dog as a threat. At the very least, a jogging trailing dog who enters the territory of another dog can elicit protective instincts. This puts you and your dog at risk of being attacked. Encountering loose, aggressive dogs can happen when a dog who normally stays in his own yard gets loose. It can just as easily happen in rural areas where an uncontained ranch dog sees you and your dog.

The fact that you are likely to encounter loose, aggressive dogs is one of the primary reasons it is imperative that the dog you train is friendly toward other dogs and is not protective of you. The last thing you want is an aggressive dog with hackles up approaching you, and having to worry that *your* dog is going to challenge the other dog to a fight. This is why selecting a dog that is not dog-aggressive for MAR work is important.

I strongly recommend using a backup person on actual searches and when training in public. A backup person can talk to people who ask questions while you focus on working the dog; intercept loose or aggressive dogs; and watch for traffic and potential distractions (other dogs or cats).

For safety and protection, trailing dog handlers should always work with a backup person.

I also recommend that you and your backup person arm yourselves with pepper spray. Pepper spray can stop a bear (or other wild animals), is carried by most postal workers, and is dispersed as a liquid. There are also citrus-based dog repellants that are supposed to be safe and effective at stopping a charging dog. I do not recommend mace because it is an aerosol and there is a greater risk that it will drift back and affect you. I know of a MAR trailing dog handler who has her backup person carry an air horn so she can startle any charging dogs and disrupt an attack.

The subject of hazards that you might encounter during lost pet searches is covered in Missing Pet Partnership's MAR technician certification course. Be aware that training and working a MAR search dog can be just as risky and dangerous as training and working a dog for search-and-rescue work. Anything can happen, and you are safer by working with at least one trained person who can help protect you and your dog.

Training Logs

I strongly recommend that you document the training of your MAR dog by keeping a training log. Training logs are used with traditional SAR dogs to evaluate the progress (and mistakes) made during training and to help the SAR dog handler determine when their dog is ready to move forward in their training program. These logs typically record the date, time, temperature, wind conditions, terrain, age of trail, length of trail, and a narrative description of how the dog performed. Training logs for SAR dogs can sometimes be requested in a court of law when the handler is asked to give testimony about their search dog's qualifications.

The Laci Peterson investigation is a perfect example of a simple missing persons investigation where a search-and-rescue dog's training was scrutinized by a court of law. Although your chances of being asked to go to testify in a criminal court are minimal, it is possible that you might be asked to assist by tracking a lost pet involved in a lost person investigation. Certainly a MAR trailing dog could have been used in the Laci Peterson investigation to retrace the path of the family dog (who Laci supposedly took for a walk).

I was once asked to use my MAR trailing dog to track the scent of a horse during the investigation of a woman who disappeared while riding her horse. I've also been used to search for a missing cat that vanished during the commission of a homicide. You just never know when your animal tracking skills might become interwoven into a missing person or criminal investigation.

Although unlikely, it is also possible that your training or the work with your MAR dog could be called into question in a civil lawsuit. Anyone can sue you at anytime, and having proof of how much training you have invested with your dog is one way to help protect yourself.

You can find samples of training logs on-line. I personally recommend that you use the *Search and Rescue Canine Trailing Log and Journal* by J.C. Judah (available through www.dogwise.com) because it helps you keep your dog training information together with other vital information (MAR certifications, MAR contacts, lost pet investigation documentations, etc.).

Chapter 9

CAT-DETECTION TRAINING

If you have a dog who has passed a MAR evaluation (see Resources) and is excited about kitties, then you can move forward in training him for cat-detection work. Follow the information in the previous chapters, especially the basic training covered in Chapter 8; next comes training to detect the scent of cats. If you follow this step-by-step plan, you will soon be ready to offer your services as a pet detective.

Step 1: "Check This"

The "Check this" cue is used to teach a dog to sniff a particular area. You use this cue during a search when you ask the dog to sniff under a deck or bed, in a drain pipe, and other areas where a lost pet could be hiding.

Begin by dropping a treat on the floor a few feet in front of the dog. Tap your finger next to the treat as you say, "Check this." Repeat this several times a day. Then transition to tapping on a spot where you placed a scent. To do this, take a piece of hot dog and smear it on the ground so the hot dog leaves an oily spot. Tap your finger on the hot dog scent and give the "Check this" cue. Right as the dog sniffs the spot, reward him. If you are using a clicker, click and treat as soon as he sniffs. If the dog responds to a toy, then toss him a toy as you praise him. If he only responds to praise, then praise with excitement as he sniffs where you tap. Practice this cue by placing treats in tall grass, in bushes, and under decks and crawl spaces. Initially, the dog learns that the "Check this" cue results in a reward. Teaching the dog to sniff on cue in bushes, under decks, and in unusual spots will prepare him for sniffing for cat scent when conducting an area search.

Tap your finger next to the treat as you give the "Check this" cue.

Next, use different food scents (tuna, peanut butter, etc.). Dab the scents high on a wall so the dog must stand on his hind legs to reach the scent. Tap on the scent and click and treat when he stands up and sniffs the spot on the wall. As he sniffs, add the cue, "Check high," whenever he stands on his hind legs to reach the spot on the wall. This teaches him that you want him to stand on his hind legs to sniff. Finally, dab the scent even higher and in unusual places so the dog must climb onto a table or a couch to reach the scent. The dog might one day need to climb onto a workbench in a garage and stand on his hind legs to sniff the rafters for the scent of a cat. Diversify the "Check this" and "Check high" training so the dog becomes accustomed to sniffing wherever you point while standing on various footing.

Once the dog does well in "Check this" training sessions, point to a location where there is no food or food scent. When the dog sniffs, praise him and give him a treat, or click and treat. Eventually, you will move away from giving treats to saying, "Check this," when there is no treat, *no* scent of a treat, and the reward for the dog will be just verbal praise. At this stage you will use treats occasionally for varied reinforcement.

Since the "Check this" cue will be used on all future lost-cat searches, it is important that the dog responds consistently. Periodic maintenance training sessions throughout the dog's working career will ensure a high response to this cue.

Dab hot dog scent high on a wall so the dog must stand on his hind legs to sniff.

Step 2: "This Way"

Conducting an area search involves frequent changes of direction. Even though the dog is attached to a long lead connected to a harness, you need to control his movements with voice cues and hand signals. The "This way" cue teaches the dog to look to you for a hand signal that communicates the direction you want him to move. This cue is used only for cat-detection dogs and dual-purpose dogs while they conduct area searches. It is not necessary to teach this cue to trailing dogs.

The "This way" hand signals consist of extending your arm out straight, parallel to your side, while walking in the direction that you are pointing. Thus, to move the dog to your right, you point to the right while walking to your right as you give the cue, "This way."

To begin, you need a toy or treat that the dog will retrieve or eat. Have an assistant hold the dog by the collar as you stand ten yards away, facing the dog. Show the treat or toy to the dog and call his name; make sure his attention is locked on you. With the dog watching you, throw the treat or toy about ten feet away to your right. You should create a triangle: you at one corner, the assistant with the dog at the second corner, and the toy at the third corner. Hopefully, once you've tossed the treat or toy, the dog will focus on the item and not on you.

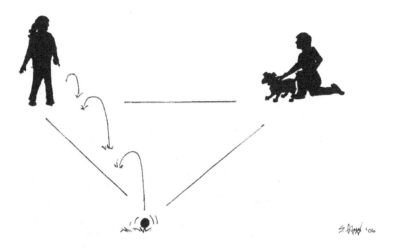

Create a triangle: you at one corner, the assistant with the dog at another corner, and the toy at the third corner.

You want the dog to look at you as you give the cue and the hand signal. As the assistant continues to hold the dog, call his name to get his attention. Right when the dog looks at you, hold your right arm out to your right and start walking to your right (your dog's left) and give the cue, "This way." Your assistant should release the dog right when he hears the words, "This way." The dog should run and grab the toy. Repeat this exercise several times, switching back and forth between throwing the treat or toy left or right as you give the proper hand signal.

Once the dog has learned the cue, you can reinforce it whenever you're walking together outdoors or when the dog is loose in the yard. When the dog is distracted, walk in a different direction from the dog. Give the "This way" cue in an excited voice, walk in the opposite direction and extend your arm in the direction you are walking. The dog should abandon what he's doing, look at you, see the hand signal, and change directions.

Hold your arm out and walk in the direction of the toy as you give the "This way" cue.

Be sure to practice the "This way" cue when the dog is wearing his harness connected to a long lead. Begin walking with the dog, and allow him to move forward and investigate a scent. When he is distracted, walk in the opposite direction as you give the hand signal and the cue. The dog soon learns to look at you when you change direction. Eventually, the dog automatically turns and changes directions without even looking at you when you give this cue.

Practice the "This way" cue when the dog is wearing his harness connected to a long lead.

Step 3: "Where?"

The next step is teaching the "Where?" cue. This cue is used when the dog has detected a scent. The goal is to encourage the dog to find the source of the scent he's detected by using an excited tone in your voice. Teaching the "Where?" cue involves games similar to the search games outlined in Chapter 8.

Take the dog by his collar, ask him, "Are you ready? You wanna work?" then toss a piece of hot dog in front of the dog (where it's visible to him), give the "Search!" cue at the same instant that you let go of his collar. The dog should rush forward and eat the treat, at which point you praise him. If he's not food motivated, use a knee-high nylon stuffed with cat fur.

After a few training sessions of throwing the hot dog where it is visible, move to an area where the hot dog is hidden after you toss it. *You* should know exactly where the hot dog lands because you must know when the dog has picked up the scent. Find a patch of tall grass, weeds, or some type of ground cover that conceals the treat. However, be careful not to throw the treat into plants or bushes that might be toxic or harmful to the dog. Educate yourself about the plant life (oleander, poison ivy, fox tail stickers, etc.) in the area that is harmful to you and the dog. If you live in an area where there is no ground cover, then toss the treat behind a couch, hedge, or barrier that blocks the dog's view.

The dog should use his nose to search for the hot dog. When the dog first detects the scent, you are likely to see a change in his body language. He might jerk his head, change directions, or sniff rapidly. This indicates an "alert," a physical indication that the dog detects a scent. Right as you see this alert, give the "Where?" encouragement cue by drawing out the word into a long "Wheeerre?" sound. Just as the dog makes the find (and gobbles the hot dog), click and praise. Do not give him another treat; finding the hidden treat is the only food reward in this exercise.

At this point, the dog is probably ignoring you and is focused on one thing: using his nose to find the treat. By using the "Where?" cue right as the dog picks up the airborne scent, you teach the dog: "I want you to *pinpoint* that scent you've just picked up." You use the "Where?" cue in advanced training when the dog hits the scent cone of a cat in a crate. On actual search missions, when you see the dog alert as he catches a whiff of scent, you can ask him, "Where?" and encourage him to take you to the source of the scent that he has detected.

Step 4: Imprinting

Imprinting is the process used to teach a dog to focus intensely on a certain scent. If you are training the dog to find drugs, you imprint or expose him to the odor of marijuana. If you are training the dog to find firearms, you expose him to gunpowder, gun oil, and gun cleaning solvents. But because you've chosen to train a MAR cat-detection dog to search for missing cats, you imprint the dog to the scent of cats. Imprinting requires the repetitive exposure of a scent combined with praise, food rewards or games with the goal of creating a strong desire to find cat scent.

The first step in imprinting is to obtain a target cat and a small cat carrier. You want to use a target cat who is not afraid of dogs. The cat should be accustomed to being transported from home and being kept in a crate for hours at a time. The ideal cat is one who is relaxed while crated, a cat who does not meow or make noise. Your goal initially is to teach the dog to use his nose, not his ears, when searching for a missing cat. (Refer to Chapter 4 for details on how to select and train a target cat.)

The first training sessions should be conducted outdoors. Be sensitive to the weather conditions and the welfare of the cat. Do not hide the cat when it is extremely hot or cold. The target cat should have access to food, water, and a litter box *before* the training session. When hiding the target cat, use a black cloth and mesh cat carrier like those made by Sherpa or Tutto. Dogs are less likely to use their eyes and more inclined to use their noses to pinpoint the location of the cat if you use these types of carriers.

You must teach the dog to associate a cue word with cat scent and, hopefully, create excitement for cat scent. You develop that passion based on how you present the scent and the experience to the dog. Since you've decided to train the dog in cat-detection work, he probably shows an intense, friendly interest in cats, making it easier to teach him to have a passion for cat scent. Eventually, you will teach the dog to detect and signal when he finds the scent of deceased cats.

When selecting a cue word, you can use those I suggest in this book or select your own. Be sure to be consistent and clear when you give cues. When teaching a dog to search for cats, I use the cue word, "Kitty." When imprinting a dog to a particular scent, you first let the dog encounter the scent, then immediately give him the cue word followed by the reward once the object is located. When using the cue word, be sure to use it in an upbeat, positive, drawn out sound: "Kit-teeeee, kit-teeeeee" or "Kitty-kitty-kitty-kitty-kitty." Your primary goal is to excite the dog with the cue word as he detects the scent.

You already know what rewards the dog responds to. I learned what type of reward my dogs wanted based on their reactions to what I offered. My dog, Rachel, always wanted to play a game of tug-of-war with a stick. After she made a find, she would hunt for a stick to pick up. My Bloodhound, A.J., refused to play with a toy or eat treats. A.J. simply wanted direct eye contact and to have his chest rubbed. My Bloodhound, Chase, and my Whippet-mix, Kody, both wanted a food reward when they made a find. Be sensitive to what the dog wants and be sure that you pour it on when he finds the scent you want him to search for!

Make the first session of imprinting short and positive. Place the crated cat outdoors in a safe, comfortable location. If possible, set the crate where a light breeze carries the air scent and creates a scent cone. You want the dog to pick up the scent of the cat as far away from the crate as possible. Your goal is to imprint the dog with the cue word immediately when you determine that the dog picks up the scent of the cat. Begin by walking the dog toward the crate, preferably directly into the wind. This should put you directly into the cone of the cat's scent, which is blowing toward the dog from the crate.

You should be able to tell by a change in the dog's body language that he has picked up the cat scent. He might turn his head, lift his nose, wag his tail, ignore you, or sniff rapidly and move toward the crate. This body language is an alert, and is the precise moment when you want to say, "Kitty-kitty-kitty." You want the dog to hear the cue word as he detects the scent and works toward the source. If the dog does not lead you toward the crate, you should lead him toward it.

Your verbal praise ("Good booooooy!" or "Goooooood girrrrllll") should come precisely as the dog arrives at the scent source, in this case, the cat in the crate. Once the dog arrives at the crate, praise lavishly.

If the air is still and there is no cat scent drifting toward the dog, you might need to walk the dog near the crate before he alerts. As soon as he picks up the scent, immediately say, "Kitty," and follow up with praise. Once he realizes there's a fuzzy kitty inside the crate, he should go wild with excitement.

Repeat this same exercise, moving the cat each time (at least twenty yards) and concealing it in a different area. If there is no wind, allow the cat to sit for another ten minutes so a large pool of scent can build up by the crate. If there is a good breeze, move the cat and start the process over again.

Work no more than four short sessions at a time, always ending on a positive note. Be sure to vary training locations and target cats to avoid boredom and to get your dog accustomed to new locations. Hide the cat at parks, in the woods, under houses, and around industrial buildings. If the dog shows a lack of excitement after the first or second session, stop. I recommend that you do some type of (short) scent training like this at least four days a week.

You will notice a difference in the dog's body language when he first picks up the airborne cat scent and when he actually sees the kitty inside of the crate. Most likely, the dog will sniff rapidly when he picks up the airborne scent, then stare, whine, and wag his tail when sees the cat. Take note of what you see. Observe the dog's body language carefully. More than likely, it won't be the last time that you see this body language. Does the dog whine? Does his tail wag? Do his ears perk forward? Ideally, the dog should have a dramatic and intense level of excitement. A dog with a dramatic alert is the easiest dog to read when working on actual searches.

Every cat-detection dog has his or her own individual body language. When my Weimaraner, Rachel, detected a live cat, she moved in jerky, quick movements with her head and body low to the ground. When she pinpointed the direct spot where a live cat was hidden, Rachel would freeze in place and wiggle her tail rapidly. If I noticed a few rapid tail wiggles during the search, it usually meant that she had picked up airborne scent particles from a cat in the area, sometimes from the yard next door.

My other Weimaraner, Sadie, would wag her tail while whining loudly when she found a kitty. Susie, a Jack Russell Terrier cat-detection dog I helped train through Missing Pet Partnership, had a dramatic change in body language when she picked up cat scent. Her pace increased, her perky ears went flat, her tail wagged rapidly, and she whined and whimpered as she frantically worked to find the cat. Once she pinpointed the kitty, Susie's entire body wiggled as she dipped and cried to entice it to come out and play. Through consistent observation, you will eventually learn to read how *your* cat-detection dog reacts to the scent of cats.

Cat-detection dog, Susie, would wag her tail, flatten her ears, and whimper when she detected the scent of a cat.

Step 5: Crated Cats

By now the dog has imprinted on kitty scent, understands that the cue word "Kitty" means cat, and has learned what it means to "Search!" You're now ready to teach the dog to search for a hidden cat.

Pick a training location (a nearby park, school, shopping center with bushes) in an area where you're fairly certain that there is no cat scent. Use an assistant who can help you hide a target cat and monitor him (to make sure no one disturbs or takes the cat). Leave the dog in your car or with an assistant, and hide the cat in some bushes or in an area where the crate is completely concealed.

To teach a cat-detection dog to find an object you've hidden, you first walk around and deposit your scent throughout the entire search area. You can do this by walking and touching different objects before you hide the cat. Walk in circles, in zig-zag patterns and spend several minutes walking into areas where you didn't carry the crate. Otherwise, if you simply walk up to one spot and set down the crate, then walk back along the same path, the dog soon learns to cheat by simply following *your* scent trail to where you hid the cat. However, if your scent (or your assistant's scent) is dispersed throughout the entire search area because you've walked all around and touched different objects, the dog learns to ignore your scent and focuses on finding the cat scent instead.

After the cat has been hidden for at least ten minutes, harness the dog and prepare to work him. Hold him by the collar, give the "Are you ready? You wanna work?" cue followed by the "Search!" cue right as you release his collar. Walk behind the dog. Use the "This way" cue with directional hand signals to direct the dog where you want him to search. Have him check areas as you point and give the "Check this" cue. As you walk along, also use the cue, "Find the kitty," periodically to help the dog focus on cat scent. Once you are near the crate and you see the dog's body language change (alert), use the encouragement cue, "Wheerrrre?" to praise and encourage him. Once he finds the kitty, lavish him with praise, treats, and perhaps even a chance to play with the kitty if the target cat cooperates.

Step 6: Find and Paw

The dog should now be ready to work at finding a cat that is inaccessible. The purpose of teaching this is to make certain the cat-detection dog will paw at the scent of a cat he can't reach. If you direct him to sniff a shed door or the screen at the base of a house, he should paw (push) at that door or screen if he detects cat scent. The dog will learn to paw through repeated training exercises in which you hide a cat the dog can detect, but can't reach due to a physical barrier.

To teach a dog to paw, you need to hide a crated target cat and leave her unattended for at least one hour. Make sure you are only training during nice weather and that the cat is secure in a hard plastic carrier. Do *not* use a cloth carrier because (trust me on this) the cat can chew a hole through the mesh door and escape!

Hide the target cat inside a shed (right by the door) or under a house right next to a crawl space. To make certain that the target cat isn't distressed, place a baby monitor (transmitter) next to her crate and listen (with the receiver) for meowing. Wait for at least one hour for a significant scent pool to form. Harness the dog and walk him through the area on lead. Ask him to "Check this" at various spots before you lead him to the shed door or screen, and give the same "Check this" cue. When the dog alerts with excitement, encourage him, but wait for him to paw at the shed door or the screen on his own. If he doesn't paw on his own, give the "Push" cue, and praise him when he paws at the door or screen. Take out the crated cat, and allow the dog to play with the kitty if possible.

You now have the basics for training a cat-detection dog. You're ready to move on to advanced training problems.

If your dog jumps with joy when he detects cat scent then you're ready to move on.

Step 7: Advanced training

At this point, you're ready to put together all training steps, including the "Check this" and the "This way" cues, as you work advanced training problems. Hide a target cat in an area that is several hundred yards from where you plan to start the dog. Assign a volunteer to watch the cat to make sure he's not disturbed by loose dogs or someone who mistakenly thinks the cat was abandoned.

Give the dog the "You wanna work? Ready? Search!" cues in an area where there are bushes or areas of concealment, but no cats. Point to various bushes and hiding places, and ask the dog to "Check this" as you praise him. Change directions and use hand signals as you cue, "This way." You condition the dog to listen to you when you instruct him to change directions frequently.

Next, move toward the area where the cat is hidden. Allow the dog to locate the cat's scent and to find the cat. Make him paw at the crate (give the "Push" cue if needed). When he makes the find, reward him with praise and, if possible, take out the target cat and let them play (harnessed and on-lead). After the dog has a chance to interact with the cat, give him a food reward or play with him if he wants to play with a toy.

Train in new locations that offer distractions. Search for a cat in a busy shopping center parking lot with bushes, shopping carts, cars, people, and other strange scents and sounds. Train near or on a ranch with horses, cattle, and other strong animal odors. Ask permission from family, friends, and neighbors to train on their property so you can work the dog in different yards, under different conditions. Train where the dog can learn to ignore barking dogs on the other side of a fence. Train while it is snowing or raining so the dog doesn't wimp out in bad weather. Hide several target cats so the dog can find one, you praise him, and then tell him to "Search!" and get to work and find the second or even a third kitty.

Advanced training includes teaching the dog to use his ears to find a meowing cat. To do this, use a cat who has not been trained to sit in a crate quietly. Borrow a cat who is not afraid of dogs, but who does *not* want to be in a crate and who will meow. Don't use a cat who is afraid of dogs because this traumatizes the cat and could result in a nasty encounter between the two. Hide the meowing cat and work the dog toward the area where he is hidden. Watch the dog to see a physical response when he hears the meowing. Use the "Wheerrrre?" cue to encourage the dog, and offer praise as you allow him to use his ears (and nose) to find the hidden cat.

Slowly extend the amount of time the dog searches before he finds the kitty. Initially, work the dog for ten to fifteen minutes before he locates the cat. Eventually, you want to work the dog for forty-five minutes to one hour, and eventually two hours, before you find cat scent. Give the dog a break and drink of water every twenty minutes or so, especially in warm weather. This conditions the dog for actual searches in which you take breaks and sometimes search for two hours without finding a cat.

Set up situations in which the dog finds the target cat when she is loose, not in the crate. Do this exercise only where the target cat is contained: in a house, garage, or warehouse. Be sure the dog is on lead. For dual-purpose and trailing dogs, you can also walk the cat on a harness attached to a lead to leave a scent trail to a hiding place (the crate). With this method you have to allow a harnessed cat to lead the way while you simply follow and end up with a scent trail that is determined by the cat. Another method of laying a cat scent trail is to place a crated cat on top of a skateboard equipped with a handle (I prefer the Switchboard Scooter & Skateboard model made by Fisher Price). This way you can actually control the route of the scent trail by wheeling the cat from start to finish.

Prior to certification, the dog should be trained to detect and find cat decomposition scent. (Read about decomposition scent training in Chapter 12.) On-the-job training comes after the dog is trained (and certified) while working on actual lost-cat cases. Even when working a certified cat-detection dog, you should still set up occasional training problems to increase the dog's proficiency and correct any problems that you encounter on actual searches. Before long, you and the dog will find and save the lives of lost cats, bringing great relief to owners who are grateful for your services.

Chapter 10

TRAILING DOG
TRAINING

While cat-detection and dual-purpose dogs are trained in scent detection and used to search an area for a scent, trailing dogs are trained in scent discrimination. Trailing dogs are taught to focus on one scent and ignore the scent of other people, dogs, cats, and animals while they are working. If a trailing dog encounters a loose dog while trailing the scent of a missing dog, he is trained to continue with his work. While trailing dogs usually search for lost dogs, they can be used to search for any pet (including cats) that travels significant distances or has been displaced.

MAR Technician Landa Coldiron and her Bloodhound, Ellie Mae, follow a scent trail through a park.

A major difference between an area-search dog (cat detection and dual purpose) and a trailing dog is how the dogs react to the presence or absence of scent. When you work an area-search dog, you search areas that may or may not contain the missing pet's scent. You work in no-scent or low-scent conditions, and watch for the dog to alert to the sudden presence of a large volume of airborne scent. But when you work a trailing dog, you always begin with the presence of the missing pet's scent at the point he was last seen (Point A) and hopefully follow it to where the pet is located (Point B). After presenting the trailing dog with the target scent, you work the dog and watch to see if (or when) he runs out of scent. (*See Diagram 8*)

Socks for Scent Article Transition Training

I suggest using socks initially to teach trailing dogs to sniff scent articles because they are visible, lightweight, absorbent, and dispensable. At first, use a clean (rather than scented) athletic type sock because it is only a visual cue designed to teach the dog to associate tossing a sock in the air with the excitement of runaway games.

Okay, I admit using socks sounds quirky, but here is how I developed the technique. After spending several years observing Bloodhounds being trained to find people, I noticed a common transitional problem. Many of the hounds were giddy with excitement when the trail layer teased them and took off running to hide. But when the handler advanced to the stage in training where the hound no longer watched the person lay the trail but rather was simply presented with a scent article (t-shirt with the trail-layer's scent) laid out on the ground, many hounds were uninterested, others clearly confused. After the handlers presented them with the scent material, these hounds just bumbled about.

Based on the excitement I initially witnessed in previous runaway games, it was obvious that the dogs had no idea that they were supposed to follow a scent. I believe this is because the hounds did not make the connection between the t-shirt lying on the ground and a person hiding in the woods. That is why I developed a scent article transition method using socks that results in a dog who is excited to see a scent article (initially a sock) lying on the ground. *Trailing dogs need to understand that a scent article lying on the ground means they are about to work a scent trail.* You want to develop a dog who will drag you with excitement in an effort to sniff the scent article. Training the dog to associate the scent article with

Diagram 8

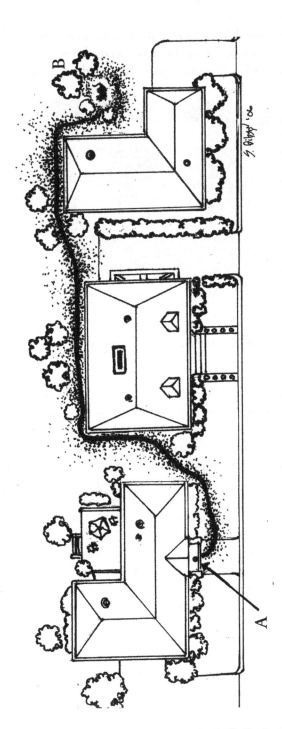

Trailing dogs can be scented at the escape point (Point A) and follow the scent trail to where a displaced cat is hiding (Point B).

the trail is probably the most critical aspect of training a trailing dog. (If this piques your curiosity, skip to the end of Step 11 to read a summary of how the sock is eventually phased out of the training process.)

Trailing dogs should drag you with excitement in their efforts to sniff a scent article.

Collecting Scent Material

When collecting scent from another dog for training purposes, use a sterile gauze pad and wipe the target dog on his sides, back, face, ears, tummy, and anal gland area. Sterile gauze pads are bacteria-free. They can be used to wipe pet dishes, toys, bedding, or other objects to collect the pet scent that you present to the dog in actual searches. You and the target-dog handler should wear rubber or latex gloves when collecting the target dog's scent to avoid contamination. Although the trailing dog is likely to ignore your scent, the target-dog handler should not touch the scent material for any reason. If the target-dog handler touches the scent material, it is considered contaminated and could easily confuse the trailing dog. You want to make sure that the dog understands he is to follow the target dog scent and not the target-dog *handler's* scent.

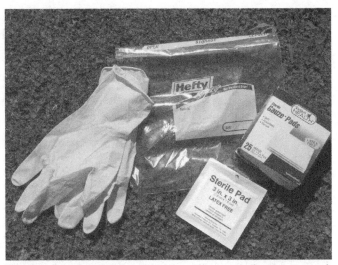

Wear gloves and use sterile gauze pads to collect scent from a target dog.

Wear latex gloves to collect scent material and an entirely different type of glove (leather, for example) when actually working the dog. Tracking gloves are needed to protect your hands from blisters when the trailing dog pulls strongly on the lead, sometimes for hours. My personal preference is the soft leather, batting gloves made by Franklin. They are available in sporting good stores and sporting goods section of many department stores. The Franklin brand is just the right thickness, is comfortable, and offer some protection from injuries during search work. However, these leather gloves absorb and retain scent—animal and human—creating a risk of cross-contamination of one scent article with another. Thus, it is best to use rubber gloves to prepare the scent article, then place it in a sealed plastic bag. After the scent article has been bagged, you can put on the leather tracking gloves.

The best way to bag the sterile gauze pad and other scent articles is to use a gallon-size, sealable, plastic bag. If the scent article is small enough (e.g., dog sweater, dog brush, cat toy, cat collar, etc.) to fit inside a gallon-size bag, then you can present the article instead of the gauze pad to the trailing dog. Avoid picking up the article with your gloves; instead, use the same method used to pick up dog feces with a plastic bag while taking a potty walk. Open the bag, and with your gloved hand push the bottom of the bag inside out and pick up the scent article with your hand that is inside the bag. You should be able to pull the scent article into the bag and seal it without touching it directly.

Push the bottom of the bag inside out and pick up the scent article.

Pull the scent article into the bag without ever coming into direct contact with it.

Ask the pet owner which items contain *only* the scent of the missing pet. Avoid items that contain the scent of other pets. If you use an item that contains the scent of another pet or animal, especially if that pet's scent is distributed outdoors, you dramatically reduce the chance that the trailing dog will pick up the correct scent trail. Collect scent from crates, bedding, food dishes, collars, hairbrushes, teeth-cleaning items, toys, or other objects that contain only the scent of the lost pet. Use a sterile gauze pad to wipe scent from items and then place the gauze into a plastic bag and seal it.

Most scent articles contain some of the owner's scent; dog dishes, collars, toys, and blankets or bedding are touched by owners at some point. Through proper scent discrimination training, the dog learns to ignore the human scent and focus on animal scent. To make a trailing dog's job easier, select scent articles that have the least amount of human scent, such as pet bedding that has not been changed for a while or a dog brush in which you collect scent from the bristles (not the handle). If you're lucky enough to have access to a sweater or other canine clothing, collect the scent from the inside; the interior that is in direct contact with the lost dog's body. Since a pet owner typically touches the outside of a garment, you increase the chance of presenting a strong scent of the lost pet to the trailing dog using this technique.

Trailing dogs are notorious for cheating: sniffing the closed or unzipped plastic bag (that contains the scent article) before you're even prepared to hook them into their harness. If this happens, go through the process of scenting the dog directly on the scent material anyway, but don't be surprised if the dog immediately starts to work and seems to ignore the scent material. For this reason, I recommend that you keep the dog in a crate, collect the scent material, set it down and close the bag at the place that you determine is the start of the trail. *Then* remove the dog from your car, harness up, walk him and let him sniff around the area (and urinate if necessary) for a few minutes, scent him on the article, and work the trail.

Now that we have covered the role of scent articles and how to collect them, you can begin to work with your trailing dog to follow the scent successfully. I have divided the training into many steps to benefit the novice trainer. Trainers who have experience in tracking or search-dog disciplines may be able to skim through some of the following steps.

Step 1: "Take Scent" Cue

Before you actually work scent trails, you need to teach the dog the "Take scent" cue. This exercise teaches the dog to stop and sniff the scent article before he takes off on a scent trail. It's a quick training exercise that you can do every day, especially on days that you don't have time to work an actual trail. This cue is taught separately from trailing training and is incorporated into trails (Step 4).

To teach the dog the "Take scent" cue, you need a sterile gauze pad and a treat with a strong odor: pieces of hot dog work well. If the dog tries to nibble the gauze pad, rub the gauze pad on a strange dog, cat, or on other animal (e.g., snake or turtle). The idea is to have a scent that intrigues the dog enough to make him want to sniff. Even cat or dog feces scent might do the trick. Do not use any strong chemical scent, perfume, or anything that is too powerful or harmful to inhale.

Hold the dog by his collar in one hand and place the gauze pad under his nose. Right as the gauze pad is under his nose and he is able to smell the scent, give the "Take scent" cue. Praise him as he sniffs the gauze pad. Repeat this exercise, but use a new gauze pad with a different scent. If you present the same scent a second time, you run the risk that the dog becomes bored with it or may only associate the cue with a particular scent. Keep the scents intriguing and varied, and the dog will be eager to sniff the gauze pad when you present it to him.

Place the gauze pad under the dog's nose and give the "Take scent" cue.

Some trailing dog handlers prefer to present all scent articles to their dogs by lifting the item up rather than placing the item on the ground. If you teach the scent article on the ground method, make sure that you always set it on plastic so that it does not come into direct contact with the ground. If you elect to use the scent article on the ground method then you need to teach the dog to sniff an object on the ground when you point at it. Instead of holding the sterile gauze pad and bringing it up to the dog's nose, set it on the ground on top of a clean garbage bag or a gallon-size plastic bag. While holding the dog by his collar with one hand, point and/or tap at the gauze pad with the other hand as you give the cue, "Take scent." Let the dog strain forward against his collar to sniff at the gauze pad, but don't release him. Praise and reward him as he sniffs the gauze pad. If you use a clicker, click and treat right as he sniffs the gauze pad.

Next, transition from a gauze pad to placing a scented sock down on a garbage bag or on a gallon-size plastic bag. The sock should be a clean sock that you rubbed over a strange dog (find a friend or neighbor who lets you collect their dog's scent for this purpose). You can also fill a sock with dog fur collected from your groomer. This gives the sock an intriguing smell that the dog should want to sniff. Or, try rubbing the sock with hot dog or other food smell that encourages the dog to sniff. If the dog is treat crazy, you might even put a treat directly on top of the sock, point or tapping at it, and give the "Take scent" cue right as the dog eats the treat. This helps condition the dog to sniff the sock because he expects a treat.

If the dog is mouthy and tries to pick up the sock to play or run with it, secure it so that he cannot pick it up. Use two strips of duct tape and tape the sock to a plate. The beauty of taping the sock to a plate is that it makes it nearly impossible for the dog to pick up the sock. It quickly teaches him to use his nose and not his teeth. Once the dog learns that you want him to sniff the sock and take off on the scent trail, you can eliminate the tape and plate and go back to only using the sock.

Step 2: Short Trail With Sock Throw

This step involves short, brief, hide-and-seek games between the trailing dog and the target dog. Work this step at a location that has plenty of trees, bushes, buildings, or even cars that offer many areas for hiding. Because I live in a city and do not have access to a wooded area, I often train in a large shopping center parking lot, at a school or university, or in a business complex. In shopping centers, I ask the target-dog handler to run and hide behind parked cars (always be careful when working around traffic). At unoccupied schools or at business complexes, I ask the target-dog handler to run and hide behind a building. When I am able to train in the woods, I ask him to run down a trail and hide behind bushes or trees.

I recommend that you use two or three pairs of clean white socks and place them inside of a gallon-size plastic bag. You want the scent article to be visible to the dog, and heavy enough so it can be tossed into the air and not blow away when dropped on the ground. Clothing fibers tend to retain scent longer than hard objects. Socks, especially the infamous missing-a-partner-sock, are usually plentiful and expendable should they be lost or left behind.

Before training, put on a pair of rubber gloves, remove the socks from the bag and turn them inside out. This ensures that if there is another person's scent on the outside of the sock, that scent now is turned inside. Next, rub each sock over the target dog to deposit the target dog scent onto the socks. Be sure to rub the sock around the target dog's face, ears, belly, and anal gland area. Give the target-dog handler the scented sock and whatever treats you want him to use to reward the trailing dog. Since the target-dog handler's scent is deposited along the scent trail, too, it is critical that the target-dog handler wear rubber gloves when handling the scented sock. Keeping target-dog handler scent off of the scent article helps the trailing dog learn to associate the animal (target dog) scent with the target animal he's supposed to find.

The first trail the target-dog handler lays should be a fast, straight sprint for a short distance (less than 50 yards) with a sharp turn where the handler and target dog duck and hide (*see Diagram 9*). Plan ahead with the handler so he understands what to do and where to hide.

In these early stages of training, do not harness the dog until you and the target-dog handler are both ready to run the trail. The trailing dog needs to learn that the only time he wears a trailing harness is just before, during, and after a trailing session. Once you've advanced to using a gauze pad as a scent article (Step 10), the dog is likely to have made the association of the harness with trailing. Once this occurs, you can harness the dog anytime, even before you load him in the car for a training session.

Diagram 9

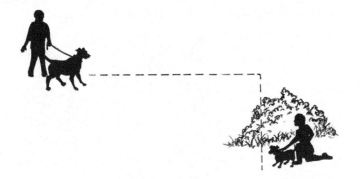

The target-dog handler and target dog run a straight trail, then duck and hide behind bushes.

With the trailing dog in harness and attached to a long lead, have the target-dog handler bring the target dog on lead so the dogs can play with each other for thirty seconds. If this is not possible, let the handler bring the target dog within a few yards of the trailing dog. The target-dog handler teases the trailing dog by calling him while you hold him by the collar.

Next, the target-dog handler backs away, and gets the dog's attention by waving the sock (rubbed with target dog scent) around in the air as he excitedly calls, "Come on, come on," and backs away. Teasing should last for only five seconds. Then, the handler throws the sock straight up high into the air at the same time that he spins around and takes off running away from the trailing dog.

While the target-dog handler teases the trailing dog, you hold onto the collar (not the harness) and encourage the trailing dog in an excited tone with words like, "Watch him, watch him!" Allow the trailing dog to watch the target-dog handler and target dog as they disappear. The trailing dog should be focused on the pair and appear eager to go find them. Ideally, the trailing dog jumps and squirms, even barks and tries to break loose from your hold because he's so excited. Holding the collar and not the harness prevents him from spinning around (and from facing the wrong direction) and keeps him focused on the target dog. The level of enthusiasm exhibited by the dog is typically a reflection of how much he loves trailing work, how committed he is to finding the scent once he loses it, and how easy it is for you to read his body language.

The target-dog handler waves the sock and teases the trailing dog.

Target dog and handler turn and run away after throwing the sock in the air.

Immediately after the target-dog handler and target dog have disappeared from view, give the cue, "Search!" in an excited tone, release the trailing dog's collar and allow him to run forward. Run along directly behind him, holding onto the long lead. The trailing dog should find the target dog easily because he will run to where he saw the pair disappear. Allow the dog to play with the target dog for a moment, then praise and reward the dog with a treat or toy.

Play two to four of these brief, fun runaway games five days a week for at least two weeks before you advance in training.

Step 3: Short "L" Trail

Please note that these early steps are all very short trails with very fresh scent. Initially, the preliminary exercises are designed to teach the dog various components of trailing. Before he learns to work advanced trails, the dog must first learn that he should sniff the scent article, that he's searching for another dog, and that there's a fun reward at the end of the trail.

This next step in training is critical. The trailing dog will learn to use his nose to find the target dog. So far, the trailing dog has *watched* the target dog run off and hide, and the target dog has always been right where the trailing dog saw him hide. But in Step 3, the target-dog handler and target dog will disappear around a corner, and travel another short distance, and *then* hide.

Diagram 10

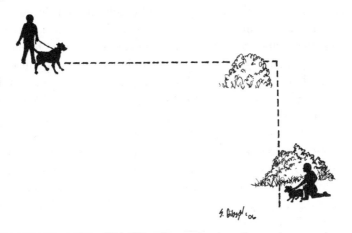

An L-trail is a trail in which the target-dog handler and target dog run a straight trail, make a sharp turn, run a short distance, and hide.

The most critical aspect to this part of training is that you must know exactly where the target-dog handler runs, and where the handler and the target dog hide. Discuss and plan ahead with the target-dog handler before you unload the dogs from the car. Or, if you trust the target-dog handler and have good communication with him, you can plot out short L-shaped trails as you work the trailing dog as long as you are clear where the handler intends to hide. These are called "L- trails" because they have just one turn and they are shaped like the letter "L" (*see Diagram 10*).

First, allow the target dog to play with the trailing dog. Then the target-dog handler backs up a few steps and teases the trailing dog by frantically calling him and waving the sock as you restrain him. The target-dog handler should then toss the sock straight up into the air, spin around, run straight ahead with the target dog, make a sharp turn around the corner of a building, and run a brief distance where they hide in a des-ignated location (behind a bush, around a second corner, behind a shed, etc.). Fifteen seconds after they've vanished, give the cue, "Search!" in an excited tone right as you release the trailing dog's collar and allow him to run forward as you run behind, holding onto the long lead attached to his harness. If the trailing dog watched the target dog run away, he should have no problem. He will run and turn the corner.

The next part is fun to watch. After two weeks of playing runaway games, the dog is expecting the target dog will be right around the corner. Be-cause you've played many runaway games with a reward at the end of the trail, the trailing dog will want the target dog to be right there! But because the target dog is farther away and hidden, the dog must use his nose to find him. As he searches for the target dog, encourage him. Don't allow the trailing dog to stray too far away from the scent trail, but ask him in an encouraging voice, "Where is she? Find her. Where is she?" as he uses his eyes and nose to locate the hidden target dog. As soon as he finds the target dog, *really* praise and reward him. Work two to three L-trails at least four times a week. The dog might have difficulty at first, but he should quickly catch onto the game of using his nose to find the target dog on the second leg of the L-trail. You should work trails like these for at least two weeks before you transition to Step 4.

Step 4: Short "L" Trail With Sock Sniff

The next transition is the trailing dog sniffs the sock on the ground before you release him to search. By this time, you've already taught the dog the "Take scent" cue at home as a separate game and he should sniff a sock when you point at it.

To protect the sock from contaminating scents from the ground, spread out a clean tarp and cover the ground where the sock will be tossed. Have the target-dog handler (who is wearing gloves) run an L-trail and toss the sock (which is saturated with the target dog's scent) up in the air as usual, making certain that it lands on the tarp. Immediately after he and the target dog disappear from sight, lead the trailing dog by his collar to the scent article on the tarp. Tap the scent article (sock) with your finger using the "Take scent" cue. Because you've already taught this cue, the dog should strain to smell the scent article. Of course, he might be intrigued with the target dog scent and linger to keep sniffing. If this happens and he spends too much time sniffing the article, encourage him to get to work until he leaves the scent article and looks for the target dog.

If you have problems like the trailing dog picks up the sock in his mouth or he spends too much time sniffing the article, switch to lifting the article up to his nose and see if that eliminates the problem.

In most cases, the trailing dog learns to sniff the article, then immediately goes to work on following the scent trail. Over time and repeated training sessions when given the scent that matches the scent trail, trailing dogs learn to make the association of "smell this scent" and "follow the matching scent trail."

Work these L-trails with the sock trails for at least two weeks before you transition to Step 5.

Step 5: Cover the Eyes Before Sniffing Sock

Next, cover the trailing dog's eyes right before you scent him on the sock. Covering a trailing dog's eyes is an effective technique that prepares the dog for when he no longer watches the target dog run away. You can use your body to block the dog's view, but this requires that you face the dog, which means you miss watching the target dog handler as he disappears around the corner.

Prepare to work an L-trail as you have on previous L-trails:

1. Target-dog handler and/or target dog plays with the dog

2. Target-dog handler teases the trailing dog

3. Target-dog handler tosses the sock in the air as he turns and runs away with the target dog

4. Target-dog handler turns the corner with the target dog

5. Target-dog handler, with target dog, ducks and hides

Immediately after the target dog vanishes around the corner, count to ten. Next, walk the trailing dog to the scent article and ask him, "Are you ready? You wanna work?" Next, cover his eyes for two seconds, then give the "Take scent" cue as you point to the sock, allowing the trailing dog to sniff the sock. Give the "Search!" cue as you release his collar and let him work to find the hidden target dog.

Cover the trailing dog's eyes right before you scent him on the sock.

By now, the dog is working short trails to find a hidden dog. He understands that his harness means he's searching and a stationary sock lying on the ground before him is something that he sniffs before he takes off running. Although he probably does not understand that the dog scent on the sock is always his instruction as to which dog he is to search for, he at least understands that smelling the sock is a part of the process.

Work trails like this for at least two weeks before you move up to Step 6.

Step 6: Cover the Eyes as Target Dog Runs Off

In this step, cover the trailing dog's eyes right as the target-dog handler and target dog run away to hide. The target-dog handler tosses the sock in the air (which lands on the tarp), spins, and runs away with the target dog. As they take off, cover the eyes of the trailing dog to prevent him from seeing where the target dog makes a turn on the L-shaped trail. After removing your hand from the trailing dog's eyes, lead him to the sock, give the "Take scent" cue, allow him to sniff the sock, and release him as you give the "Search!" cue so he can drag you to find the hidden target dog. There is no need to cover his eyes a second time (before you scent him on the sock). You did that in Step 5 simply to condition him to having his eyes covered and to work toward weaning him from needing to see the target dog.

You should spend time working on Step 6 because these trails build confidence and excitement in the trailing dog. You should work these trails for at least three weeks before you transition to Step 7.

Step 7: Target Visible, Hides Around a Corner

By now the trailing dog understands the search game, and is happy and excited to play it. This particular step weans the dog away from seeing the target-dog handler and target dog run away. The dog sees them briefly, but only right before the target-dog handler tosses the sock. I like to make this transition at a school or an office complex that has multiple buildings because you can use the building corners to run a series of three particular trails.

The target-dog handler stands in plain view of you and the trailing dog, with the target dog by the corner of a building just a few yards away from the harnessed trailing dog. The target-dog handler should call and tease the trailing dog, and duck around the corner of the building. The target-dog handler and target dog are only yards away, but now they are not visible to the trailing dog. The target-dog handler calls the dog, then tosses the sock in plain view of the trailing dog. This sock tossed into the air should excite the trailing dog and cue him that he's about ready to search.

The target dog prepares to hide around the corner of a building.

The target dog prepares to hide after the sock is tossed.

After tossing the sock in view of the trailing dog, the target-dog handler should go a short distance and hide while you briefly cover the trailing dog's eyes. Then, lead the dog to the sock. By this time in training, the trailing dog is probably dragging you so he can sniff the sock on the ground. Give the "Take scent" cue right as the dog sniffs the sock, followed by the "Search!" cue, release his collar, and allow the dog to drag you around the corner to find the hidden target dog.

The target dog hides and the trailing dog is ready to search.

Work on these hide-around-the-corner trails for at least two weeks before you move on to Step 8.

Step 8: Target Out of View Around a Corner

Next, the trailing dog no longer sees the target-dog handler and target dog. This is an important step and a milestone because you're almost ready to work trails that have been aged. Aged trails are trails on which significant time (hours or days) has passed between the time the target dog was walked and the trailing dog works the scent trail (see Step 20).

With the trailing dog in your car or secured out of sight, the target-dog handler takes the target dog and hides around the corner of a building. They should only be yards away from where you start the trailing dog, but they are silent and out of the trailing dog's sight.

Unload and harness the trailing dog. Walk ten yards toward the corner of the building where the target-dog handler and target dog are hiding. It is important that the trailing dog is looking forward so he can see when the sock is tossed into the air. Tease the dog, saying, "Are you ready? You wanna work?" and then signal the handler by saying, "Okay, now." When the target-dog handler hears you say, "Okay, now," he should make a noise (stomp the ground, bang lightly) and immediately toss the sock into plain view of the trailing dog. Trailing dogs typically lurch forward with excitement when they see a sock tossed from around the corner like this. This confirms that the dog associates the sock with the runaway game. After tossing the sock in view of the trailing dog, the target-dog handler and target dog should turn and run a short distance, and hide as you cover the trailing dog's eyes (as part of the game) for five seconds. Then, lead the dog to the sock, give the "Take scent" cue as the dog sniffs the sock, give the "Search!" cue, and allow the trailing dog to find the hidden target dog.

Work these target-dog-hidden-around-the-corner trails for at least two weeks before you try Step 9.

Laying Scent Trails

Congratulations! Once you've completed Step 8, you're ready for the target-dog handler and target dog to lay scent trails. When training police Bloodhounds, the term "laying a trail" means that the person who the hound will hunt (known as the trail layer) goes for a walk, depositing scent as he walks. When training MAR trailing dogs, laying a trail is the same, except that the trail layer is the target dog and the scent the trailing dog follows is the scent of the target dog. Don't worry about the fact that human (target-dog handler) scent is also on the trail because later on you will train the trailing dog to ignore it. However, be certain that the target-dog handler scent is not on the scent article.

When laying a scent trail, the handler and target dog are no longer running away from the trailing dog. In fact, the target-dog handler should walk the target dog while the trailing dog is in your car and, at later stages in advanced training, while the trailing dog is napping at home.

Step 9: Sock in Plastic Bag Lying on Ground

Before you advance to working aged scent trails, you need to make a few transition steps related to scent articles. With the trailing dog crated, the target-dog handler walks the target dog and lays a scent trail that you let age for about fifteen minutes. Find a park bench or somewhere the target-dog handler and target dog can sit and wait for you and the trailing dog to find them. You should know exactly where the target-dog handler and target dog walked, where they turned, and where they are hiding. Start with trails that are about one block long, but have at least one sharp turn or change of direction. Give clear instructions to the target-dog handler so you know where the trail is. I recommend using walkie-talkies so the handler can notify you if he had to deviate from the planned route, and so you can communicate questions if the need arises. If you lay the trail in a residential area, you can always follow the target-dog handler in your car to observe which side of the street he walked on and where he turned.

Follow the target-dog handler and target dog to observe where the scent trail was laid.

Another option is for you (trailing dog handler) to walk along with the target-dog handler (and the target dog), then retrace your path back to the start of the trail. This is a last resort because if you lay too many trails like this, the trailing dog learns to cheat and follow your scent to find the target dog. Also, be sure to switch target-dog handlers periodically so that the trailing dog does not associate the same human scent with all of the target-dog scent trails. It is equally important to occasionally use new target dogs that your dog is not familiar with.

With the target-dog handler and target dog in place, remove the trailing dog from the car. Allow him to walk (on-lead) the area for fifteen minutes. Let him walk around in the immediate area and sniff where the target dog walked. This occurs on genuine lost dog cases, so the dog should be accustomed to snooping around and encountering scent to which you later cue him to follow.

Next, harness the trailing dog. If you have an assistant (someone other than the target-dog handler), have that person hold the dog. If you are alone, tie the dog to a pole or tree for a moment. Take the sock, scented with the target dog's scent that's inside of a gallon-size plastic bag, and set it on the ground. Open it up so the sock is inside the bag, but exposed so the dog can sniff it. Do not lay the sock directly onto the ground because there could be other scents on the ground that could contaminate the scent article or distract the dog.

Expose the sock so the dog can sniff it, but don't place it in direct contact with the ground.

Lead the trailing dog to within a few yards of the sock, place your hand over his eyes for five seconds, remove your hand and move forward to allow him to sniff the sock as you give the "Take scent" cue. As he sniffs, give the "Search!" cue and immediately release his collar (while holding the long lead) so he can work the trail. Follow him as he works the trail and reward him when he finds the target dog. You have now transitioned from games to working actual scent trails. If you plan to train the dog in dual-purpose work, then this is the point at which you can introduce cat-detection work. Refer to Chapter 11 for details on dual-purpose training, and how to differentiate trailing work from cat-detection work. Continue to work these fresh trails while still using the sock as the scent article for about a week before you move on to Step 10.

Step 10: Gauze Pad in Plastic Bag on Ground

Now you can age trails for around thirty minutes. You can read about setting up aged trails in Step 20. It is also time to wean the trailing dog away from socks and transition to sterile gauze pads that are scented with the target dog's scent.

Before the target-dog handler lays the scent trail, put on a pair of latex gloves and wipe the target dog with a sterile gauze pad. Collect scent from his face, ears, tummy, and under the tail. Place this gauze pad in a gallon-size plastic bag.

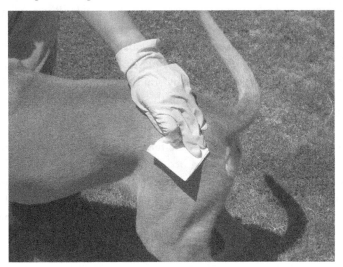

Swipe the target dog with a sterile gauze pad.

The target-dog handler walks the target dog and lays a trail. You should know exactly where they walked and where they are waiting. Wait thirty minutes, then harness the trailing dog. Hook the thirty-foot lead to the tracking harness and have an assistant hold the dog or tether him while you set up the scent article. Open the plastic bag so the gauze pad is exposed, making it easy for the dog to sniff, and lay it on the ground at the beginning of the trail. Lead the trailing dog to the gauze pad, cover his eyes for a few seconds, remove your hand and move forward, letting him sniff the gauze pad as you give the "Take scent" cue. Give the "Search!" cue right as he sniffs and immediately release him so he can work the trail.

At some point, usually after you've reached the step of setting the gauze pad on the ground, covering the dog's eyes can be dropped from the process. Covering the dog's eyes was only a transition cue used to wean him away from seeing the target dog and, later, from seeing the sock tossed in the air. Stop covering his eyes once he consistently drags you to the scent article.

Step 11: Various Articles Inside Plastic Bag

The final step in scent article training involves using a variety of scent articles that contain the target dog's scent. When working actual investigations, I sometimes use a sterile gauze pad (that I've wiped over an object that contained the lost pet's scent) as my scent article. But a dog collar, dish, or sweater saturated with the lost dog's scent makes a great scent article and I use them whenever they're available. On some occasions, the scent article is too big to place into a plastic bag, such as an entire doghouse or a giant dog bed. This is why you should use the gauze pads, plus a wide variety of objects that contain the target dog's scent when training and during actual searches.

Use scent articles saturated with the target dog's scent, such as a dish, a collar, a blanket, a toy, or a dog bed. Vary your training, using a sterile gauze pad one day and a dog blanket with the target dog's scent the next training session. If you don't like the dog to sniff the article as it lies on the ground, lift the scent article to the dog's nose. Pick whichever method you want to use, and then use it consistently with that dog.

Also, you should only use a sterile gauze pad as your scent article (and not the actual scent article) if there's any chance that more than one trailing dog will be used on an investigation. That's because when you allow the first trailing dog to sniff an object, his scent will then become transferred onto the article. This contamination can easily confuse a second trailing dog who might pick up the scent of your trailing dog and follow it instead of the scent of the dog.

You can also lift up the scent article to the dog's nose instead of setting it on the ground.

So far, you've worked through the fundamental steps needed to train a dog to work a basic scent trail. But the journey has only just begun. Now it's time to age trails several hours, add distractions, scent discrimination, vehicle trails, and other complicated exercises.

Scent Article Transition Recap
Before reading on, here's a recap of the progression of scent article transition you use to train a dog to smell a particular scent and follow a matching scent trail.

- **Sock is tossed in the air during a runaway game.** The target-dog handler tosses a sock straight up in air as she turns to run away with the target dog. You restrain the trailing dog until the target dog is hidden. Once the target dog is in place, give the "Search!"

cue and release the dog who is then allowed to run past the sock to find the hidden target dog. At this stage of training, the trailing dog is not expected to sniff or do anything with the sock.

- **Trailing dog is asked to sniff a sock.** The trailing dog knows the "Take scent" cue (Step 1). When preparing for the next level, the handler tosses the sock straight up in the air just as she turns to run away with the target dog. Restrain the trailing dog until the target dog is hidden. Once the target dog is in place, lead the trailing dog to the sock lying on the ground. Give the dog the "Take scent" cue as you point at the sock, allowing him to take a quick sniff of the sock. Release the dog's collar and run with him as he finds the hidden target dog.

- **Cover the dog's eyes before sniffing the sock.** The target-dog handler tosses the sock straight up in the air just as she and the target dog turn to run away. Restrain the trailing dog until the target dog is hidden. Once the target dog is in place and before you and the trailing dog move toward the sock, place one hand over the trailing dog's eyes to block his vision for five seconds. This step slowly prepares the trailing dog for when he no longer sees the target dog run away. After removing your hand from the dog's eyes, lead him to the sock, give the "Take scent" cue, allow him to sniff the sock, give the "Search!" cue, release his collar, run with him, and praise him when he finds the hidden target dog.

- **Cover the dog's eyes as the target dog runs away.** The target-dog handler tosses the sock straight up in air just as she and the target dog turn to run away. Immediately cover the eyes of the trailing dog to prevent him from seeing where the target dog makes a turn or hides. After removing your hand from the dog's eyes, lead him to the sock, give the "Take scent" cue, allow him to sniff the sock, and give the "Search!"" cue as you release his collar and run with him to find the hidden target dog.

- **The target dog is visible, a sock is tossed from behind a corner, and the dog's eyes are covered.** The trailing dog associates the sock tossed in the air with the excitement of runaway games. You know this for sure when you transition to this step. The target-dog handler stands by the corner of a building with the target dog, visible to all. The target-dog handler calls and teases the trailing dog, then, with the target dog, ducks behind the corner of the building.

The target-dog handler counts to five and tosses the sock into plain view of the trailing dog. The trailing dog will, hopefully, lurch forward with excitement when he sees the sock tossed in the air. The target-dog handler lays a short trail with a turn and hides as you briefly cover the trailing dog's eyes. You then lead the trailing dog to the sock, give the "Take scent" cue as he sniffs the sock, give the "Search!" cue as you release his collar, and run with him as he works to find the hidden target dog.

- **The target dog is not seen at all, a sock tossed from beyond a corner, and the dog's eyes are covered.** This next step is a transition to wean the trailing dog from seeing the target dog. It enables you to age trails and work advanced trailing problems. With the handler hidden behind the corner of a building, hold the trailing dog by his collar and signal the target-dog handler that you're ready (i.e., yell, "Ready!"). The handler makes a noise (stomps his foot, clicks a clicker, etc.) to attract the trailing dog's attention. It is critical that the trailing dog look in the direction of where the target-dog handler is so he can see the sock as it is tossed in the air. The trailing dog should lurch forward, become frenzied, or show some level of excitement when he sees the sock tossed from behind the building. Momentarily cover the trailing dog's eyes, lead him to the sock, give the "Take scent" cue, allow him to sniff the sock, give the "Search!" cue as you release his collar, and run with him as he works to find the hidden target dog.

- **The sock is lying on the ground, and the trailing dog is in the car.** The trailing dog no longer has to see the target dog (and target-dog handler) to successfully find them. He associates having his eyes covered briefly with the sock lying on the ground. Thus, the next step is to have the target-dog handler and target dog lay the scent trail before the trailing dog is taken out of the car. Both target-dog handler and target dog are hiding in place and you know exactly where they walked (they no longer need to run). You then place the sock covered with the target dog's scent on the ground (on top of a gallon-sized plastic bag) at the start of the trail. You then walk the harnessed trailing dog a few yards behind it, place your hand over his eyes for a brief moment, then point at the scent article, give the "Take scent" cue as the dog sniffs the sock, give the "Search!" cue as you release him, and let him work the trail to find the hidden target dog.

- **The gauze pad is on the ground, no sock.** Once the trailing dog becomes used to working a trail without seeing the sock tossed or the target dog, it is easy to transition away from using a sock. Since you've already used sterile gauze pads in training when teaching the "Take scent" cue, now, instead of using a sock, use a sterile gauze pad with the target dog's scent. After the target-dog handler and target dog are hidden, place the scented gauze pad on a plastic bag that is on the ground at the start of the trail. Next, lead the trailing dog to the gauze pad, momentarily cover his eyes, cue him to take scent, and follow him as he works the trail. At some point, usually after you've reached the stage of setting the gauze pad on the ground, the momentary covering of the trailing dog's eyes can be dropped from the process.

- **Various scent articles.** The final step in scent article training involves training with a variety of scent articles. Instead of using only sterile gauze pads, use items that are saturated with the target dog's scent, such as a dish, collar, blanket, toy, or bed.

Step 12: Target Dog Tied to Post, Handler Hidden

To do this, the target-dog handler lays a trail with a few turns and ends the trail by tying the target dog to a tree, bush, or pole to secure the dog in place at the designated (mutually agreed upon) end of the scent trail. The target dog should be out in the open along the scent trail, making it easy for the trailing dog to find him. The target-dog handler should then hide a short distance away from the end of the trail. He should be close enough to help the target dog should he become entangled, chew on the leash, or should a stranger approach who thinks the target dog is abandoned, yet concealed from the view of the trailing dog.

The trailing dog should find the target dog before he notices the target-dog handler. If for some reason the trailing dog shows interest in approaching the target-dog handler, anchor him, and encourage him through praise to find the target dog. For more info on anchoring, refer to the "Anchoring, Leading, Pivoting" section at the end of this chapter.

The target-dog handler ties the target dog to a pole, walks away, then hides from view.

Step 13: Target Dog Tied to Post, Handler Visible

After you've worked trails in which the target dog is tied to a post and the target-dog handler walks away and hides, work a trail where the target-dog handler is visible, even walking toward the trailing dog as he approaches.

Set up a trail as described in Step 12, only this time the target-dog handler ties up the target dog and then backtracks *toward* the start of the trail from where he just came. He should approach and then stand still, within view of the trailing dog. If the trailing dog approaches the target-dog handler, the handler should ignore him. The target-dog handler should continue to walk forward, past you. If the trailing dog tries to approach the target-dog handler, anchor him so he can't approach and encourage him to get back to work to find the target dog .

The purpose of this exercise is two-fold. First, it is a test to make sure that the trailing dog is not following the scent of the target-dog handler. If the trailing dog runs past the target-dog handler and focuses with excitement on the target dog, then you know that the dog is right on track. If instead, the trailing dog is fixated on the target-dog handler, then you have some work to do. It is natural that the trailing dog might want to greet or sniff the target-dog handler because his scent is also along the trail. Many repetitions of this training exercise (anchoring to prevent interaction with the target-dog handler and plenty of praise when the trailing dog focuses on the target dog) helps teach the dog to ignore the target-dog handler. Second, when the target-dog handler walks toward the trailing dog, you also teach him to ignore pedestrians as he's working a scent trail.

The trailing dog ignores the target-dog handler who is in plain view.

A trailing dog plays with a target dog.

Step 14: Target Dog Exchanges Hands

One method used to make certain the trailing dog ignores the target-dog handler's scent is to use two different target-dog handlers who meet halfway along the trail where they exchange handling the target dog. This training session requires planning, but is easy to set up. The first target-dog handler walks the target dog from the starting point to a designated halfway point. The second target-dog handler walks from a different direction and meets the first target-dog handler at the designated point. Then, the second target-dog handler takes the target dog and leaves in a different direction while the first handler sits down on a bench and remains at the halfway point.

The first target-dog handler hands the target dog over to the second handler at a designated point.

Start the trailing dog at the beginning of the scent trail. The trailing dog should not only ignore the first target-dog handler (whose scent ends at the halfway point), but he should continue to follow the target dog scent (which is now mixed with the second target-dog handler's scent). If the trailing dog focuses his attention on the first target-dog handler and won't continue to trail the target dog, then you need to focus on scent discrimination training by working simple, short, split trails as described in Step 15.

Step 15: Split Trails

A great method for introducing scent discrimination training is to work the trailing dog on split trails. A split trail is when you have two or more people with dogs walk together, but then split up (at a designated point that you've agreed upon) and walk in opposite directions for a short distance (but hiding from the trailing dog's view). One dog is the target dog and the second dog is called a "decoy dog." You then scent the trailing dog on the target dog's scent. At the split in the trail, the trailing dog should ignore the trail of the decoy dog and pick up the correct turn to find the target dog (*see Diagram 11*).

Diagram 11

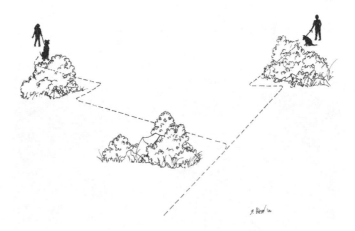

To begin, the target-dog handler and target dog, along with the decoy handler and decoy dog, stand next to each other in view of you and the trailing dog. Harness the trailing dog and place the scent material from the target dog in a gallon-size plastic bag. Use rubber gloves to collect the scent, and make sure there is no target-dog handler (or decoy) scent on the scent article. Give the trailing dog the "Watch him" cue so he watches the two people and two dogs walk off together. Cover the trailing dog's eyes as the target and decoy dogs split from each other and walk in opposite directions at the designated point. The distance between you and the split in the trail should be about twenty yards. The decoy dog and target dog, along with their respective handlers, should walk an additional twenty yards and hide so the trailing dog cannot see them.

The target-dog and decoy-dog handlers walk off together.

Scent the trailing dog on the scent material of the target dog and give the "Take scent" and "Search!" cues. Hopefully, the trailing dog makes the correct split in the trail and finds the target dog, but do not be surprised if he doesn't catch on right away. Split trails and other scent discrimination exercises can take months before a trailing dog is consistently finding the correct dog. Be patient.

If the trailing dog makes the wrong turn and heads toward the decoy dog, simply anchor him so he can't move forward toward the decoy. Encourage him to take the split and turn in the direction of the target dog, and immediately praise him when he heads in the correct direction. By guiding him toward the correct dog, you prevent the trailing dog from making a mistake. Whenever the dog takes the correct split in the trail on his own, immediately verbally praise him and follow up with a reward (treat or toy) once he finds the target dog. Eventually, he learns to use his nose to ignore the decoy dog, and to focus on getting to the target dog as quickly as possible. If you work more than one split trail, you need to move to another area that is not "contaminated" with any of the target dog or decoy dog scent.

Once the trailing dog is doing well on split trails with concealed decoy and target dogs, try a split trail in a wide-open space, such as a soccer field or playground. Do not cover the trailing dog's eyes. He should be allowed to watch the two people and two dogs walk away, split from each other and come to a stationary position approximately forty yards apart (since both walked twenty yards in the opposite direction).

If the trailing dog becomes too distracted by seeing the two people and two dogs, momentarily cover his eyes, but allow him to see both dogs and people standing in the open before you start. Your goal is to get him accustomed to scent discrimination exercises in the open where he sees both of the dogs (decoy and target) involved in the exercise.

Try doing a split trail in which the target dog and decoy-dog handlers are both visible.

Step 16: Wagon Wheel Exercise

Once the dog is accustomed to watching two dogs and their handlers walk in the open and create a split trail, you can add more dogs and people. This method of scent discrimination training is called the "wagon wheel." To do this simply add a third decoy handler with a decoy dog to the split trails exercises. Three people and three dogs (one target and two decoys) walk straight out for approximately ten yards and then they all split in different directions. One can walk straight and the other two can walk in a diagonal direction, similar to the spokes of a wagon wheel (*see Diagram 12*). Eventually, you can have five to seven dogs in the wagon wheel. Make sure the dogs are equal distances apart, approximately twenty yards from each other.

Diagram 12

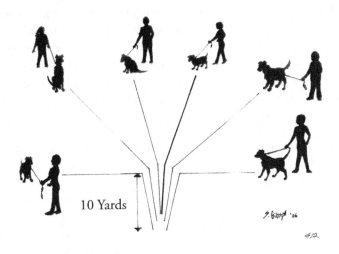

10 Yards

After the trailing dog watches the target dog, and several decoy dogs and people walk out into a wagon wheel formation, scent the trailing dog on the target dog scent. If he heads toward a decoy dog, anchor him and don't allow him to move forward. Only allow him to move in the direction of the target dog. When he does move toward the target dog, immediately praise him! Once he reaches the target dog, allow him to play, then reward him with a treat or toy.

If you plan to do more than one wagon wheel (or split trail, for that matter) in a session, make sure you move to another area of the park or field so you do not overlap scent. Also, do not work split trails and wagon wheels in an area where the target dog has already walked. For example, if the target-dog handler allows the target dog to run around the park before the training exercise, his scent would be dispersed all over the ground, making it much more difficult, if not impossible, for the trailing dog to work the exercise.

Step 17: Stationary Decoy Dog

By this time, the trailing dog has been finding target dogs for several months and is used to being rewarded for finding a dog, not a person. Next, add more people, strange dogs, and other distractions into the search area so the trailing dog learns to stick with the scent trail that matches the scent material to which he was scented. Adding decoy dogs along the trail teaches the trailing dog to ignore other dogs. This is a true test of scent discrimination: when the trailing dog learns to follow the scent trail of one target dog while ignoring the scent (and presence) of all other dogs in the area. I recommend that initially you use a decoy dog who is familiar (and not very exciting) to the trailing dog. This might be a second dog who lives with the trailing dog. Do not use a dog unfamiliar to the trailing dog. If you use a strange dog, the trailing dog might be too interested and distracted by the new decoy dog. Save new, interesting dogs for future target dogs who the trailing dog can track.

To work this exercise, the target-dog handler should walk the target dog and lay a basic, fresh trail with a couple of turns. The trail should be only one block or a block-and-a-half in length, and you should know exactly where the trail is. Once the target dog handler and target dog are in place, the decoy-dog handler should walk a decoy dog along the same route. However, make sure the decoy dog scent is not on the scent article or anywhere near the start of the trail. About midway along the trail, have them split off and move fifteen yards off the scent trail and stop. If the trail is laid in a residential area, the decoy-dog handler and decoy dog could stand on the opposite side of the street from where the target dog walked.

Then, scent the trailing dog on the scent article (which contains scent from the target dog), and allow him to work the trail. Hopefully, the trailing dog will ignore the decoy when he sees him. If not, tell him to "Leave it" and guide him back to work on the scent trail. If the decoy dog is close or is within the scent of the target dog's trail, the trailing dog might need to get close enough to the decoy dog to discover it is a different scent. Just don't let him linger or greet the decoy dog. Tell him to "Get to work" and praise him once he is past the decoy dog and back working the trail again.

Teaching the trailing dog to ignore other dogs and other dogs' scents is a process. Be patient, and be prepared to set up different decoy dog problems along the trail. You should notice that the trailing dog learns to either totally ignore other dogs or he leaves them alone much quicker.

Step 18: Decoy Dog on the Move

Once the trailing dog works trails with stationary decoy dogs along the way, have him work past a moving decoy dog. At first, let the trailing dog come directly behind a decoy dog who is walking in the same direction that you and the trailing dog are traveling.

When the trailing dog consistently works past decoy dogs who walk away from you on the trail, set up a trail in which the decoy (and decoy dog handler) dog walks on the trail directly toward you. This is more difficult because the trailing dog will see this decoy dog long before he is within sniffing distance. Chances are that the decoy dog will exhibit signals (tail wagging, staring, etc.) to the trailing dog, creating a situation in which both dogs may be focused on preparing to greet each other. Tell the trailing dog to "Leave it," and encourage him to move on, praising him when he leaves the decoy dog alone.

Step 19: Distracting People Along the Trail

When working a search dog, bystanders may want to stop you and talk to you, and pet the dog while he's working a scent. They often ask, "What's wrong?" because they see the rescue gear and want to know if a person is missing. The trailing dog must learn to ignore these people and ignore the fact that you might talk with people while he's busy working a scent.

Since you will be taking pet owners along with you when you conduct lost-dog searches, take a second person along with you as you work the dog. This helps the dog get used to ignoring other people who come along as he works his trail. It is also a very good practice to always have a back-up person with you while training and when you work searches. The back-up person can warn you of approaching traffic and loose dogs, intercept loose dogs, talk to witnesses, and motion for traffic to slow down if the trailing dog is working close to the roadway.

Finally, have the target-dog handler lay a basic trail with the target dog and take a second person with them. The second person, who the trailing dog has not seen yet, should backtrack and wait halfway along the trail. When the second person (this should be a stranger to the trailing dog) sees you and the trailing dog approach, he should kneel and start trying to interact with the trailing dog. Encourage the trailing dog to keep working and ignore the person. You can talk to the person, just don't let the dog stop and greet.

Have a stranger try to distract the trailing dog while he is working a scent trail.

Step 20: Aged Trails

Once your trailing dog is accustomed to working trails with confidence, you can start to age the scent trails. This means that several hours pass between the time the target dog walked on the trail and the time you come out with the trailing dog to track the scent trail. Initially, you work fresh trails in your training sessions, trails that are minutes old. But once you transition past runaway games, you should work on letting the scent drift, settle, and dissipate. Your confidence will build as you discover what most trailing dog handlers discover: given good trailing conditions (cool, damp weather with no wind) the trailing dog can work a twelve-hour scent trail with about the same ease that he worked a two-hour trail!

A common method of aging a trail is to have the target-dog handler lay the trail with the target dog, leave the area, and return to the ending point at a later time.

Following is a typical scenario:

- The target-dog handler and target dog are dropped off at a coffee shop at 8:00 a.m. and walk half a mile to a local park.

- The person who dropped the target-dog handler and target dog off at the coffee shop picks them up at the park, then leaves the area. The person who transports them can be you (the trailing-dog handler) or it can be someone else.

- Three hours later, the target-dog handler drives the target dog back to the park (at the end of the scent trail) where they sit and wait for you and the trailing dog.

- You, with the trailing dog, then drive to the coffee shop (the start of the scent trail that was laid three hours prior) and scent the trailing dog on the scent material of the target dog. You need to know the exact trail that the target-dog handler took, so he should draw you a detailed map of his route.

If you choose to drive behind the target dog and target-dog handler and watch as they lay the trail, you should *not* transport the target dog inside your car before you work the trail (it is fine to do so afterward). Switch cars if you have to, so that you drive a car that does not contain scent from the target dog. Cars are not airtight and scent escapes from seams, ventilation systems, and windows. By transporting the target dog in your vehicle and crossing over the scent trail laid when he walked with the target-dog handler, residual target dog scent could escape from your car, potentially confusing the scent trail.

I suggest that you work on aging trails in the following increments through the many months that you train:

1 hour

4 hours

8 hours

24 hours

48 hours

72 hours

5-day trail

7-day trail

14-day trail

You do not necessarily have to age trails in this order, but you should work on increasing the difficulty of your scent trails. Don't forget that wind and weather will affect the difficulty of the trail. Heat causes the scent to rise, often above the level of the dog's nose, tires out the dog, and destroys scent particles. In warm weather, the most optimal time to work the dog is in the early morning hours when there is moisture (dew) on the ground and the scent has dropped close to the ground. Pet detectives who live in warm climates often work scent trails starting before 5:00 a.m. during hot summer months to take advantage of the moist and cool conditions.

Step 21: Negative Trails

In addition to learning to read the trailing dog's body language when he's working a scent and then loses it, you need to learn to read what the dog's body language looks like when he's taken to a place where there's absolutely no scent from the target dog.

This training is called *negative trails*, and involves a short exercise in which you teach the trailing dog that he should give you an indication that there's no scent if he doesn't find a trail after you've given him the scent. This exercise will help teach the trailing dog that he should not just take off and pull you around on what is called a *ghost trail*.

A ghost trail occurs when the trailing dog pulls you around for the sake of pulling rather than actually working a scent. This can happen on actual searches when the handler believes, simply because the trailing dog is pulling in the harness, that the trailing dog is on a scent. Trailing dogs who have not been trained on negative trails can inadvertently learn to sniff a scent article and start pulling, even when the target scent trail is not there. This is called "sniff-and-run" behavior and is something you want to avoid. It is imperative that trailing dogs learn to stop pulling if they cannot find the scent that was presented to them. They learn this through a lot of training on negative trails.

To train on negative trails, collect scent from the target dog. Now drive the trailing dog to an area of town where you have determined in advance that the target dog has not been. The plan is to present the target dog scent to the trailing dog in an area where there is absolutely no target dog or target dog scent in the area. Scent the trailing dog on the target dog's scent and let him sniff around. You should anchor him and not run behind him freely. Make the trailing dog pull into the harness. If he insists on moving straight ahead, allow him to do this, but offer increasing levels of resistance. Your goal is to discourage him from taking off from the area when there is no scent trail, and encourage him to give "I lost the scent" body language when he has checked around and cannot find the scent.

Allow the trailing dog to check around while offering increasing levels of resistance.

When working negative trails, the trailing dog should start in one direction, but after a short distance look back or turn around to hunt in a different direction. My dogs typically travel a short distance, fifteen to twenty yards, before they circle around and check the other direction for scent. Once they've circled around (for about a minute) and can't find the scent in any direction, they eventually shake off to indicate they do not have the scent anymore. By shake off, I mean the same full body shake that dogs give after they've rolled in grass. I've never figured out why many of the dogs I've trained have learned to shake off when they're out of scent. I suspect I've shaped that behavior because although I let them check around in circles while I anchor them (offering resistance and making them pull hard into the harness as I ask, "Which way?"), I never reward them until they turn around, look at me, and shake, at which point I immediately praise them and end the exercise.

The benefit of training on negative trails is that you are eventually, after repetitive training like this, able to tell whether or not the lost animal was ever at a specific location. It allows you to check out possible sightings. This technique is often used in traditional search-and-rescue investigations when there is a reported sighting of a missing person. A trailing dog is often brought in to see if he can pick up a trail or not. You may have cases in which a pet owner says there is a possible sighting of the missing pet. You want to know if the trailing dog can indicate if the lost pet's scent is in that area. To do this, you need the assurance that if you scent the trailing dog on the missing pet's scent in an area where it turns out the pet has never been, the trailing dog won't act like he's on a scent. If you don't train on negative trails, you run the risk that the trailing dog will simply sniff and run, dragging you on a ghost trail, giving false hope and false information to a pet owner.

Negative trail exercises are something you should continue to add to your training program along with split trails, wagon wheels, vehicle trails, and, of course, aged trails with various distances. Be creative and make up new scenarios and problems that you might encounter when working an actual case. Make sure the target-dog handlers and target dogs do not lay only straight trails. Unless panicked or following the path of least resistance, dogs seldom walk or trot in a continuous straight line. They cross streets, circle, cross another street and head in different direction, and double back. While in the early stages of training, keep the trails simple and, as you advance, make the trails more realistic and difficult.

Trailing training is much more difficult than training for cat detection, but it can be very rewarding. You may not make as many physical finds with a trailing dog as you might with an area-search (cat detection or dual purpose) dog, but the trailing dog can provide valuable information to the pet owner. Through his body language, the trailing dog can tell which direction the missing pet traveled, whether or not the missing pet was ever at a particular location (confirming or discounting a possible sighting), and whether the animal was picked up by someone in a vehicle.

Step 22: Scent Trail Ends in Group of Dogs

Once the trailing dog works split trails, aged trails, turns, and other advanced problems, try working a problem in which he follows the single scent trail of a target dog that ends in a group of dogs.

For this exercise have the target-dog handler start the trail in an area where you're sure there are not many other dog scents, such as a school, shopping center, or church parking lot. Lay a trail with a few turns that ends in a large area with decoy dogs and with a lot of dog scent, such as a dog park or field where obedience classes are held. The trailing dog should ignore all of the wrong (decoy) dogs in the area and trail up to the correct (target) dog. If he alerts or focuses on a decoy dog, tell him to "Leave it!" and only praise him when he takes you up to the target dog.

Eventually, you should attempt a trail that is the opposite of this: the trailing dog tracks a scent that leaves a large group of dogs and ends with a single scent trail and a walk up find. This training simulates tracking the scent trail of a dog who escapes from a boarding kennel, dog show, agility event, dog park, or other location with several dogs where one dog escaped and is lost. It may take several training sessions, but the trailing dog will soon learn to focus on the single scent trail of the target dog whose scent is on the scent article and to ignore all other dog scent. Proficiency at this level of discrimination comes only through repetitive training around large groups of decoy dogs.

Set up trails in which the trailing dog works in and out of large groups of dogs like at a dog park.

Step 23: Lengthen Trails

Initially, training trails should be rather short, a few blocks at the most. That's because your focus is on decoy dogs, turns, aging trails, and other aspects that the dog will need to learn when working trails. But once you're aging trails (Step 20) you should also start working on lengthening the trails.

I recommend adding distance to the trails in half-mile increments. A longer trail takes longer for you to work, and requires more water breaks for you and the dog. As you add length, also consider variety. Set up a two-mile trail in which the dog works from a residential area into a wilderness, rural, or agricultural area. Set up another long trail that starts in an isolated area (wilderness, rural, or agricultural), runs next to a railroad track or a canal, and ends up at a house in a residential area.

Take water with you and purposely stop the trailing dog along the trail to give him a water break. This teaches him it's okay if you stop him along the trail. Stopping on the trail happens often when you encounter traffic, when the trailing dog needs water, and when you're interrupted by witnesses who want to talk with you. When you break, unhook the lead from the dog's harness and hook it to his collar to let him know he's off duty. Vary the length of the breaks from one to fifteen minutes. Once you're ready to work again, hook the lead back to his harness, tell him to "Get to work," and release his collar. Praise him when he picks up the scent again. You shouldn't have to scent him again on the scent article, although some handlers prefer to do so.

Actual lost-dog scent trails vary in length. Some are only a few blocks long while others go on for many miles. Be sure to vary your training trails accordingly so the trailing dog is prepared to work for several miles if necessary. At some point, the dog will be too tired to work, especially in warm weather. As you work longer trails, you will learn your dog's burnout point and know what to expect on actual searches.

Step 24: Target Dog Transported in a Car

Even though you won't teach the trailing dog to follow the residual scent of a dog who has been transported inside a car, you still need to train for this to learn how the trailing dog will react when a large concentration of dog scent dwindles down to a small amount of scent. Does the trailing dog still attempt to follow the scent, but work in the center of the roadway? Does he zigzag back and forth as he works? Does he slow down and show apprehension, but continue to work? Does he circle and appear confused? After setting up a lot of vehicle trails, you'll eventually know what the trailing dog will do when it appears that the missing pet was picked up and removed from the area.

To set up a "vehicle trail," the target-dog handler walks the target dog along a roadway. You can keep this part of the trail rather short in length. At a designated spot that both you and the target-dog handler agree on, another person in a car picks up the handler and dog. The windows of the car should be rolled up to minimize the amount of target dog scent that escapes the vehicle. Then, the target-dog handler and target dog travel by car to a designated park or location where they wait for you.

Set up vehicle trails in which a friend picks up the target dog and transports him in a car.

Start the trailing dog at the beginning of the trail. Have another friend follow behind you in a transport vehicle as you work the trailing dog. Have them stay well behind you so the car exhaust fumes don't affect the trailing dog. When the trailing dog reaches the point where the target dog was placed in the car, he will lose the scent of the target dog. Watch for any type of confusion or physical body language that looks similar to the way the dog looks when he overshoots a turn, has lost the scent, or indicates no (negative) scent. Help him if necessary by slowly anchoring him. When the trailing dog gives a negative indication, praise him and unsnap the lead from the harness back to his collar. By doing this, you teach the dog to indicate (with a negative indication) that he's lost the scent trail where the animal was picked up and transported in a car.

Next, load the trailing dog into the transport vehicle and drive to the park where the target dog is waiting. Once you arrive at the park, take the trailing dog to the car that transported the target dog to the park. Eventually, just have the target-dog handler and target dog sit and wait inside the car. That's because you want the trailing dog to find target dogs in unique places. But, initially, they can leave the car and sit on a nearby park bench. Snap the lead back to the dog's harness, give him the "Get to work!" cue in a praising voice, and allow him to follow the scent trail of the target dog into the park. Reward him when he finds the target dog. Whenever you work a negative trail, be sure to set up a short and easy ending so the dog can make a quick find and receive a reward.

Step 25: Target Dog Picked Up and Carried

A variation to Step 24 is to have a person physically pick up and carry the target dog. For the comfort of the target-dog handler, use a small dog (fifteen pounds or less) as a target dog. The target-dog handler walks the target dog, makes a turn or two, and at a designated point picks up and carries the target dog, continuing for another block to a designated point where he stands or sits, but holds the dog.

The scent of the target dog is still present, even though he was carried. But it is dispersed differently when carried. Most likely, since the dog was elevated above the ground, the scent trail is farther from the path where the target-dog handler walked. Observe the trailing dog to see if his body language changes at the point where the target dog was picked up and carried. Unlike the vehicle trail, the dog is more likely to continue to follow the scent trail of a dog who is carried by a person because there is still a large enough concentration of the scent present; it is just dispersed differently.

Set up trails in which the target-dog handler picks up the target dog and carries him in her arms.

Step 26: Scent Pools

A scent pool is an area that contains a large concentration of scent caused either by the target dog remaining stationary for a length of time or from the dog moving back and forth and all around (circling, doubling back, moving about) in a relatively small area. A scent pool is created when a large amount of scent hovers in a cloud-like manner around the source of that scent so there's no longer a single path of scent, but rather a giant area that all smells the same. Trailing dogs must learn how to work through scent pools and figure out where the subject they are trailing (the target dog) exited.

You can create a scent pool when the target-dog handler stops with the target dog along the trail and remains stationary for at least thirty minutes before continuing. You should also set up a scent pool in which the target-dog handler leads the target dog around in circles several times to deposit scent. You need to work scent pools on days when there is no wind in order to create a cloud of scent that hovers.

Keep the target dog in one place for thirty minutes or longer to set up a scent pool.

One of my favorite techniques is when the target dog creates a scent pool at an intersection. To do this, the target-dog handler walks the target dog on a straight trail through a residential area. For example, they head north on a street. When they approach an intersection (a street that runs east and west), they spend fifteen minutes walking around and around all four corners, dipping twenty yards in one direction, coming back to the intersection and going in another direction. Then, they continue walking north to where they end the trail.

When you work the trailing dog on this trail, closely observe how he works the scent. Some dogs become very confused and circle around in scent pools while others blaze right through them unaffected. You need to learn how scent pools will affect the dog. Give the trailing dog plenty of time to check around and follow the scent. Let him check out the other directions (east and west) if he wants to, but he should give you a negative indication when he ultimately runs out of scent heading too far (a half block) in those directions. If he gets stuck and can't figure it out, help by guiding him to the scent trail north of the scent pool. Praise him as he gets back on the trail and ultimately makes the find.

Step 27: Starting Off the Trail

"Starting off the trail" means you present the scent to the trailing dog where there is no known scent of the target dog. You are training the trailing dog to look for the scent trail rather than, as you have in other training exercises, start him where you know the trail begins. Before you work on this exercise, you should have already worked on negative trails. Your first attempt at starting off the trail should be simple. Identify exactly where the target dog walked and which way the wind, if any, was blowing at the time the trail was laid. Bring the trailing dog out to a spot that is about fifteen yards away from where the scent trail is located and face in the direction the target dog traveled. Present the trailing dog with the scent article and let him move forward so that he initially won't smell the target dog scent, but quickly intersects the scent trail. Praise him once you know he's picked up the scent trail and let him make the find. Once he's doing well at this, you can start him farther away and require him to circle around before he comes across the actual scent trail. If he gives you a negative indication when he's outside the scent, tell him, "Good boy," then lead him toward the scent trail and encourage him to move forward into the scent and to work the trail to make the find.

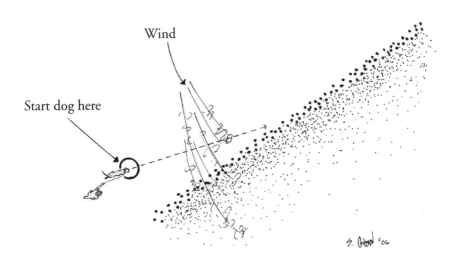

Wind

Start dog here

S. Gibson '06

One mistake that trailing dog handlers make during training is to always present the scent article within the scent of the target dog. If you always present the scent article directly on the scent trail, you will inadvertently train the dog to sniff-and-run. You have to teach the dog that sometimes the scent is right there, sometimes it's ten to twenty yards away, and sometimes it is not there at all. You teach this by negative trail training (see Step 21) and by occasionally starting him away from the scent trail during training.

Off-the-trail training is important because you will encounter actual cases in which you present the scent of a lost dog to the trailing dog at what you think is the start of the scent trail, but actually is an area where there is no scent. This can happen when you find a hole in a fence and you assume that is where the lost dog exited when, in fact, he exited through an open gate. This can also happen when you're told there's a possible sighting of the lost dog, so you respond and give the trailing dog the scent article, but it turns out the lost dog scent is down the street. In cases like these, you want the trailing dog to hunt around for the scent and then pull in the harness once he picks it up.

A neighbor of mine lost her Yorkshire Terrier. I responded two days after the escape and used my Bloodhound, Chase, who picked up a scent trail that headed north and ultimately ended at a very busy road (Shaw Avenue). I instructed the woman to post brightly colored lost-dog posters, but she didn't follow my instructions. Two weeks later, she advertised a $1,000 reward in the newspaper and received a call of a possible sighting; a terrier was just sniffing a ball in the roadway in a quiet neighborhood a mile away. I responded to the sighting with Chase. I also had my neighbor bring a scent article that contained the scent of the lost Yorkie.

The ball that the dog was supposedly playing with was actually a flattened rubber foursquare ball that didn't appear to have been disturbed. I scented Chase on the rubber ball to see if she'd pick up a trail. Chase sniffed around, dragged me a short distance, then lifted her head and shook off, turned around and checked another direction. We did this for about five minutes in which Chase checked around the intersection (this took place in a quiet residential area), but she didn't pick up a scent trail and indicated there was no animal scent on the ball. There was a clear difference between what Chase looked like when she had *no scent* compared to two weeks prior when she had dragged me along on the Yorkie's two-day old scent trail that led to Shaw Avenue.

Next, I presented the scent article that contained the Yorkie's scent to Chase. This time I was working with a known scent (of the lost dog) in order to confirm whether or not the sighting was valid and whether the Yorkie had been near the ball in the roadway, but maybe had not touched it. Once again, Chase sniffed around, dragging me for a short distance, but then shook off and indicated there was no scent from the Yorkie in that area. I instructed my neighbor to plaster posters in that area in the event that Chase was wrong and her Yorkie was, in fact, in that neighborhood.

Later that day, there was a knock on my door. It was my neighbor and she had her Yorkie in her arms! My heart sank because I immediately assumed that Chase had been wrong and that the Yorkie had been at that intersection after all (trusting a trailing dog is hard to do!). But the neighbor explained that someone who saw her $1,000 reward listed in the newspaper had called. The person had her dog the entire time at a location that was only three blocks from the neighbor's home, but a mile from the rubber ball (which turned out to be a false sighting). The person who found the Yorkie had picked him up on Shaw Avenue, just a block from where Chase lost the scent trail! A trailing dog who is trained to this caliber—a dog who is reliable in giving you negative indications—takes many, many months of consistent training.

Step 28: Correct Direction of Travel

How dogs are able to determine the correct direction of travel is unknown, but what is known is that they can determine the correct direction if you train them. Thousands of years ago, wild canids (ancestors of wolves, coyotes, domestic dogs, etc.) needed to follow scent trails in the correct direction. If they backtracked—followed the scent trail away from the direction the prey was moving—they would have starved. Backtracking is what you want to train the dog not to do. The dog will learn this through repeated training in which he intersects trails and you encourage him to take the correct direction of travel.

You train for this by setting up "T-intersection" trails. Allow the trailing dog to move forward where there is no scent (as in Step 27), intersect the scent trail at a ninety-degree angle, and make the correct turn so he follows the scent trail in the same direction that the target dog traveled.

A T-intersection is most easily set up on an actual dirt trail system so that the path that the target dog takes is narrow and well defined. If you do not have access to a trail system, then you can set this up at a school (during off hours and only if you have permission to be there with a dog) using outdoor corridors and hallways with intersecting hallways and corridors. The target-dog handler walks the target dog down the main trail (hallway or corridor). After letting the trail age for a few hours, take the trailing dog down one of the corridors where there is no scent. When you are within twenty yards of the main trail, stop the dog, scent him on the scent article, and allow him to move forward and work all the way up and intersect the scent trail.

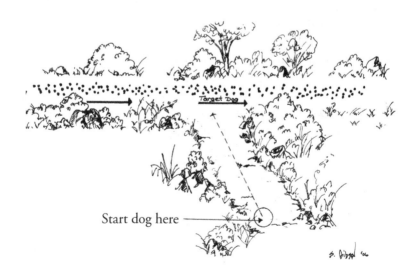

At this point, ask him, "Which way?" and see what he does. If he continues going straight and crosses over the scent trail, he will eventually run out of scent and give you a "no scent" indication by shaking off, looking at you, or whatever indication he gives when he runs out of scent. Anchor him if he goes too far and encourage him to circle back and pick up the correct direction of travel on the scent trail.

If he reaches the intersecting scent trail and makes the correct turn on his own and heads in the correct direction of travel, really praise him. If, on the other hand, he reaches the intersecting scent trail and makes the wrong turn (backtracking in the direction from where the target dog started laying the scent trail) then anchor him, and encourage him to turn around and follow the scent in the correct direction of travel (toward where the target dog is waiting).

Finally, you can work a more difficult trail by combining a starting off the trail training with the correct direction of travel training. To do this, start the dog fifteen yards off the scent trail, but intersecting at an angle that makes it very easy for the dog to backtrack the scent trail in the wrong direction. Once he arrives at the scent trail, the dog should turn himself around and pick up the scent trail so he heads in the correct direction of travel toward where the target dog is located. If he backtracks, anchor and encourage him to swing around and follow the trail heading toward the target dog.

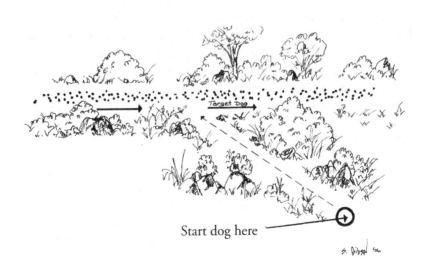

Target Dog

Start dog here

S. Dibsol '06

Step 29: Freshest Scent

The trailing dog should learn to follow the freshest scent trail during his training trails. Many cases that you work involve various scent trails that lead away from the missing dog's residence. Area-search dogs (cat detection and dual purpose) trained in air scenting already understand that they are to fix on the fresh, airborne scent as opposed to older scent that settles on the ground. When area-search dogs catch a whiff of the high concentration of the scent pool or the direct cone of scent coming from the object they're searching for, they disregard all the ground scent and use the airborne scent to help them zero in on the source of the scent.

You should teach the trailing dog that the older scent is fine to work, but that when he encounters a fresher trail with a higher concentration of scent, he should follow that particular scent trail. But let me preface this by saying that while you will train for this, the actual ability of a dog to consistently pick up the freshest scent trail when there are also older scent trails in an area is limited. That's because the dog is often rewarded for working older scent trails. Nevertheless, train for freshest scent, but understand that the chances of the dog actually picking up the freshest scent are limited. Search dogs are not miracle workers and they do have limitations!

To train for picking up the freshest trail, set up problems in which the target dog spends at least thirty minutes at a location (park, school field), leaving his scent throughout that area. Allow the scent to settle in the area for at least four days. Take the target dog back to the location and lay a single trail, leaving from the area and ending at a designated location. Allow the new scent trail to age for at least two hours. Thus, there is the target dog's aged scent (four days old) all over the park, and a distinct, heavy, fresher scent trail (two hours old) that the trailing dog will, hopefully, learn to pick up.

Adjust the age of these trails; allow the first scent to age longer. In most cases, you and the trailing dog will not respond to a search for at least a few days after a dog is missing. You should train the trailing dog on trails that have been aged for various amounts of time, in various weather and wind conditions, and over varied terrain, to prepare for real-life scenarios.

It is very difficult to track a dog who is lost from his own home if that dog was allowed to roam freely throughout the neighborhood, or if the owners routinely (or recently) took that dog for a walk. When trailing lost people, I always had a higher success rate when the person was missing from an area they were visiting for the first time versus when missing from home. For example, a child who is separated from his family while hiking in the woods is much easier to find because there is a single scent trail from the point last seen (Point "A") to where he ultimately ends up (Point "B"). Contrast this with a child who vanishes from her home. In this case, there is typically multiple scent trails that lead to and from the home (Point "A"), such as a trail from the house to school, a trail from the house to the store, a trail from the house to a friend's house, and a trail from the house to where the child ultimately ends up (Point "B"). If a trailing dog followed any one of these trails, he'd technically be correct and you'd have no way of knowing which of these trails was the freshest.

The limitations of working around multiple scent trails is an unfortunate fact all MAR handlers need to accept. Multiple scent trails left by a lost dog who is routinely taken for walks, even though they are aged differently than the freshest scent trail, could easily distract the trailing dog. You may have to take the trailing dog back to the point last seen (PLS) a second or third time to see if he works the same trail or picks up another scent trail. However, the problem in doing this is that when the dog leads you in three different directions, you're left wondering which trail is the freshest scent trail and the correct direction the dog left when he escaped. Because of my demanding schedule, I personally only worked my trailing dogs on cases in which the missing dog was not allowed to roam and was not recently walked in the area or neighborhood where he was lost.

The ideal search scenario is a dog who digs out of his yard and takes off into a neighborhood where he had not walked for months. In this case, there is a single scent trail that is much easier for the a trailing dog to trail, which gives you a much higher probability of success. Be sure to explain to your clients who routinely walk their (now lost) dog that you're willing to attempt to track their dog's scent, but your chances of success in picking up the *freshest* scent trail are fairly low.

169

Step 30: Find and Paw at an Inaccessible Dog

A final step in training a trailing dog is to have him search and find target dogs who are inaccessible, like dogs who are concealed behind a door, trapped down a well or large hole, inside a shed, or under a house. If you direct the trailing dog to sniff a shed door or the screen at the base of a house, he should paw (push) at that door or screen if the scent of the target dog he's tracking is there. Your dog will learn to paw at these areas through repeated training exercises in which you hide target dogs (sometimes loose, sometimes in a crate) who create a scent pool that the trailing dog can detect.

You need to hide the target dog and leave him unattended for at least one hour. Make sure you train only during comfortable weather, and that the target dog is secure in a hard plastic crate or is accompanied by a target-dog handler. If you leave the target dog unattended (and in a crate), you can place a baby monitor (transmitter) next to his crate and listen (with the receiver) for excessive whining or barking. I recommend leaving him with a chew toy that keeps him occupied and content. I also recommend that you only use a target dog who remains quiet while crated.

First, lay a short scent trail with the target dog that ends with him hiding inside a shed, right by the door, or under a house, right next to a crawl-space screen. Wait for at least one hour for the trail to age and for a significant scent pool to form near where the dog is waiting in a crate. Scent the trailing dog and let him work the trail, allowing him to track up to the hiding place. When the trailing dog alerts with excitement, encourage him, but wait for him to paw at the shed door or the screen on his own. If he doesn't paw on his own, give the "Push" cue and praise him when he paws at the door or screen. Then take out the target dog and let the trailing dog play with him as a reward.

Be creative in training. Lay trails of differing ages, hide the target dog under houses and decks, and even hide the target behind the door of a shed or behind the front door of a house. If possible, without causing danger to the target dog or target-dog handler, hide a target dog in a pit in the ground. The trailing dog must learn that there are searches in which he is very close to the target dog, but unable to see him. He must know to paw (push) at the source of scent to let you know that he has found the concealed dog.

More Trailing Dog Training Tips

Beyond the step-by-step program laid out above, there are a few more training tips you should be aware of and build into your plans as you move towards having your dog certified as a MAR trailing dog.

Target-Dog Handler Protocol

One of the most important components of training the trailing dog is working with target-dog handlers who can follow instructions and with whom you can communicate clearly. Nearly all trailing-dog handlers have learned the hard way that some people can follow instructions and other people simply can't! I've personally experienced the frustration of instructing a trail layer to walk two blocks, turn right, and hide behind a tree only to find that the handler walked two blocks, turned *left*, and climbed *up* into a tree! Nothing will foul up a trailing dog more than pulling him off the scent trail because you told the target-dog handler to turn right but he turned left. Confusion occurs when the trailing dog tries to take you to the left (because he knows which way the scent trail leads) and you won't let him go in that direction because you *think* the trail is to the right.

To avoid confusing trails, use target-dog handlers you can trust to follow instructions. Purchase inexpensive, portable walkie-talkies so the target-dog handler can tell you where he turns or answer questions if you are confused when working the actual trail. Follow behind the handler (while driving your vehicle) so that you can observe exactly where the target dog walks. Draw a map for the target-dog handler to follow, and give clear directions, such as, "Walk on the right side of the road" or "Stop at the park bench on the northeast corner of Fifth and Stanford, and sit for fifteen minutes to create a scent pool."

If you train in a wooded area, especially when off established trails, the target-dog handler can use biodegradable toilet paper to place on bushes or tree branches along the way, to mark the trail. You can even develop a communication system with toilet paper. A small piece of toilet paper on the ground can mean that the handler made a turn, for example.

Eventually, you will need to recruit an observer (perhaps a trustworthy target-dog handler or backup person) to help you run a "blind" trail. Running a blind trail means that you (the trailing-dog handler) will have no clue where the scent trail is. Working blind trails prepares you for tak-

When laying trails in wooded areas, the target-dog handler can use biodegradable toilet paper to mark his trail.

ing the MAR certification test and for working actual lost pet investigations in which you have no idea where the scent trail is. To work a blind trail, the observer either walks with the target-dog handler when the trail is laid or follows in a vehicle. The observer must know exactly where the target dog walked. When you work the trailing dog, the observer stays with you. Be sure the observer tells you as soon as the trailing dog moves out of the scent or has overshot a turn by fifteen yards. At that point, you can decide if or when to anchor the dog. One effective technique for doing this is to have the observer walk directly on the same path, making the same turns as the target dog. If you end up going a house length past the turn, the observer can remain stationary and tell you to "anchor!" if the trailing dog has gone too far off trail. This advanced training should only be attempted when the dog is proficient in working aged trails, has a consistent negative trail, and when you have an observer you can trust.

The success of trailing dog training depends on target-dog handlers, observers, and backup people who can follow instructions and who can communicate clearly with you while on the trail. It's important that you occasionally use different people and different target dogs in your training sessions. If you're having problems finding a family member or a friend who has a potential target dog, contact a local dog training club, place up a notice at your veterinarian's office, or recruit volunteers through a local 4-H or scout program. If you need a good backup person who is trained in first aid, tracking, and navigation skills, check with a local search-and-rescue team to see if anyone wants to volunteer to help you with training and/or actual cases. You should be able to find volunteers who love dogs, who enjoy walking (target-dog handlers) or jogging (backup person), and who can follow directions.

Anchoring, Leading, Pivoting

Anchoring the trailing dog is the process of putting tension on the lead so that you can slow him down and eventually stop him if he has worked well beyond the scent trail. Ideally, when a trailing dog runs past a turn in the scent trail, you should notice some type of change in his body language. The dog may run several yards past the turn and do something to indicate that he's lost the scent. His head might come up higher, his tail might change position, he might move to the other side of the path, he might make eye contact with you (when he normally doesn't), or he might shake. You eventually want the dog to stop on his own, turn around, and hunt for the turn he missed. Anchoring is a tool that is used to teach the dog to stop and turn around when he runs past a turn in the scent trail.

When training, add turns in the scent trails so you can teach the dog that the scent trail changes directions and he must figure out which direction the scent went. Anchoring teaches the dog that once he misses a turn in the scent trail and wanders where there is no scent, he can turn himself around, search, and find the strong cloud of scent again.

Anchoring is used to teach the trailing dog to turn around once he loses the scent trail.

Be careful not to lead the dog. *Leading* the dog means that in training sessions you control where the dog goes and you make him stick right on the trail without allowing him to overshoot turns. Overshooting turns is how you teach the dog to turn around (by anchoring him when he is out of scent) and find the scent again. Usually, handlers who lead their dogs think that by making the dog stay on the trail, the dog learns to follow the scent. I have even seen this technique encouraged in a tracking book. The suggestion is that by holding the dog close to the trail, the dog learns to follow the track scent. However, in trailing dog training the concept is that you allow the dog to overshoot his turns for a short distance so that he can learn (through anchoring) how to turn himself around and find the scent again. Training like this prepares the dog for real-life searches and increases your chances of success.

Once the dog is advanced in his work, it is good to slow and question him at intersections and turns in trails throughout the training process; you offer resistance, but then move forward with him if he continues pulling you forward. I use a "Which way?" questioning cue whenever I offer resistance. I make sure that I do this often while training so my dogs are accustomed to it. However, you need to be careful that the dog does not think "Which way?" is a cue telling him to turn around. To prevent this from happening, use the resistance cue when training on straight stretches of the trail. In an area where you know that the target dog walked a relatively straight path, slowly anchor the dog by offering increasing resistance, ask him, "Which way?" but allow him to continue moving forward. Immediately release the heavy resistance and move forward with the dog while praising him. At other times when you reach a turn in the trail, anchor, question, "Which way?" and praise the dog when he makes the correct turn.

Anchoring at corners is something you may or may not have to do in your initial training with the trailing dog. It varies from dog to dog. If you have an extremely motivated dog, chances are that he may run to chase down the "missing dog" and may blow past the turn. You may notice him starting to slow down, turn his head and look confused. When this happens, ask him, "Which way?" You might even find that he turns himself around and goes back to find the turn on his own. If he does this, really praise him.

When you work the trailing dog on a training trail, allow him to initially work past a turn and continue straight for a short distance without slowing him down. Once he's trotted past the turn and has traveled about one house length, offer resistance on the lead by anchoring and slowing him down. At this point, use the cue, "Which way?" If he continues to drag you, offer more resistance until you have totally stopped the dog from moving forward. If you've trained enough on negative trails (see Step 21), the dog should give you a negative trail indication when he runs past a turn. If he does, praise him and encourage him to turn around so that he heads back toward the scent trail. You can do this through *pivoting*.

Pivoting means that even though you don't allow the dog to advance forward in the wrong direction where you know there is no scent, he's allowed to go back the way he just came. By standing stationary, the dog can turn around and head back toward the scent trail that is somewhere behind you. Once he swings back to where you know the scent trail is, immediately praise him and, if needed, guide him until he gets back on the strongest scent trail.

Anchoring, pivoting, and working a scent trail are difficult to describe in a book or even in a classroom. If you ever have a chance to attend and observe a search-and-rescue or police Bloodhound seminar in which trailing dogs are being trained, you can learn a lot about trailing dogs. Some Bloodhound seminars are only open to law enforcement officers or SAR personnel, but others do allow civilian observers to attend. These seminars are geared for training dogs to trail the scent of people, not lost pets. I suggest that you attend only to observe. More SAR dog teams are becoming receptive to the concept of including MAR dogs in their training circles, but many are not. You also might be able to observe SAR training sessions in your community if you volunteer to be a "victim" by hiding from the local search dogs.

Missing Pet Partnership includes novice to advanced MAR K-9 training opportunities at their regional training seminars. This means that seminar participants will participate in a combination of classroom pet detective training and outdoor dog training. The Resources section in this book lists training opportunities as well as a list of recommended MAR K-9 instructors who offer MAR training services.

Final Notes

Once the trailing dog is trained and certified, and you've worked him on actual cases, plan on training him in a regular maintenance program. Do this by setting up challenging training trails at least once a week and by training with experienced MAR dog trainers whenever you can. All professional search-and-rescue dog trainers know that training does not end with certification, and this applies equally to MAR dogs. The dog's talents and your talents for recovering lost pets will continue to improve the more that you consistently train the dog, month after month, year after year.

If at any time during training your dog does not seem to respond to the training or if he seems confused, take a step back and go back to the basics. I have known advanced search dogs who became bored with long searches. Going back to the basics for a few training sessions quickly helped rebuild motivation in these dogs.

Be patient with the training process. While it's possible to train a cat-detection dog to detect the scent of lost cats in just a few months, training a trailing dog (and dual purpose dog) to follow the scent trail of an animal is a long process that takes twelve to eighteen months of hard, consistent work. I mention this as a warning because there are currently a few sources who claim to have trained (and self-certified) their dogs to track the scent of lost pets in just two months. There's even a pet detective who claims one of their dogs learned how to track lost dogs simply by observing other tracking dogs! If you research the training of police Bloodhounds and traditional search-and-rescue trailing dogs, you will discover this truth: training a dog properly to follow a scent trail using scent discrimination techniques is not a speedy or easy task. Just because we live in a society that wants instant results does not change the fact that it takes a significant amount of time to train a trailing dog.

While some people have rushed into pet detective work using dogs that are improperly trained, more and more handlers are taking the time to fully train their dogs before they ever deploy them on searches.

Consider the following e-mail from Cathy Orde, a dog handler with over six years experience in training and handling search-and-rescue trailing dogs (and drug-detection dogs). Orde came to Fresno for a MAR trailing clinic and I was able to watch her work Zoe, her Golden Retriever.

Orde invested considerable time in training Zoe to trail lost pets and was recently asked to use Zoe to track a lost dog. Here's the details of how Zoe performed on that search.

Hi Kat,

At 6:15 p.m. today I received a phone call regarding a dog that broke free from its owner when the dog saw a fox. The dog took off at 1:00 p.m., dragging its leash. The owner drove after the dog (she is having total hip replacement tomorrow), and then he took off into the trees. This is an area with sagebrush, woods with thick underbrush, numerous creeks and a river.

Neighbors had been looking for Elway, the little Bichon Frise, with no success since 1:00 p.m.. Finally, someone told them about Zoe; that's when we were called in.

I took Zoe to the PLS: she was scented and picked up the trail and trailed Elway three-fourths of a mile where she located him hung up in the rocks (steep bank) on a mountain river bank. He was very close to being strangled from his leash after it was caught on the rocks above him. It didn't take Zoe long to find him. It was interesting where Zoe trailed; I could tell the little guy was out on an adventure. I scooped him up in my arms with Zoe nuzzling him and then untangled the leash. Zoe was so happy to find him, her tail was wagging like a propeller!

We were walking down the road toward the owners' house holding Elway when the owner drove up. She was crying and so happy that Zoe found Elway. She hugged Zoe and me, then she cried even harder. She did say that she felt she would never see Elway again. There are mountain lions that hunt along this river and they have been known to take small dogs, plus there are numerous coyote packs.

Happy ending!

Cathy

Pet owners deserve to have access to talented MAR dogs like Zoe, dogs who have proven their trailing skills through extensive training, testing, and actual investigations. Eventually, national standards and certification tests will be widely available that will make it difficult for poorly trained dogs and untrained pet detectives to find work in this emerging industry. Take the time to train your MAR trailing dog properly and you'll increase your chances of having a trailing dog that will perform just like Zoe did!

Two Dogs, One Trail

You might have the opportunity to work two different trailing dogs on the same lost-dog scent trail if you decide to train (and utilize) more than one trailing dog, or if you partner with a second pet detective and work cases together. Recently, two successful MAR Technicians from Southern California, Landa Coldiron (www.lostpetdetection.com) and Annalisa Berns (www.PetSearchAndRescue.com), have teamed up to work their trailing dogs in order to solve lost-pet investigations. Here's how Landa described one of their recent successes when their two trailing dogs, Ellie Mae and Lilly, helped to recover two lost dogs, a Pekinese and a Pug.

> We're so excited. All our training is paying off! Two dogs, a Pekinese and a Pug, wandered out together through an open gate and were missing for three days in Azusa, California. The owner had no leads. Ellie Mae was scented on the Pug's collar and took off. She went about six blocks with various turns and headed into a school field where she indicated interest under the opening of a fence. Lilly was then scented on the Pekinese's collar and she ran a similar trail to Ellie, but some of it was on the other side of the street, again leading into the school field where she also showed strong interest.
>
> We conducted a thorough investigation, which included going to the school office and asking what activities were at the school on Sunday (the day both dogs disappeared). The receptionist was very helpful and told us an adult soccer league played there on Sunday. She gave us the number of the person who scheduled the soccer events. We called him and yes, he had seen people playing with a Pekinese and Pug and he knew the man who had picked them up and took them home!
>
> With our coaching, the owner called this man. Amazingly, he did not want to give the dogs up. She explained that they were older with health problems, they were greatly loved by the family, and there was a large reward! The man reluctantly agreed to meet nearby. Annalisa and I were staked out down the street, taking down license numbers of cars that came down the street just in case this guy changed his mind. We also had our binoculars out so we could see incoming people.

The man showed up and the exchange was made. We were laughing and crying at the same time. The two dogs had been transported from the school that day about one-half hour away East on the 210 Freeway to another town in an entirely different area code. The owner commented that without our canines and investigative work, she never would have found the dogs that far away. — Landa Coldiron

Coldiron and Berns trusted that both Ellie Mae and Lilly would each follow the individual dog (the Pekinese or the Pug) that they were asked to and not each other because both dogs trained together for this exact scenario on a regular basis. In order for you to achieve this level of trust, you need to make sure that your trailing dog does not learn to cheat to find the target dog (or lost dog) simply by following the scent trail of the other trailing dog that works before you work your trailing dog. To do this, be sure that you collect two scent articles from the target (or lost) dog, one for each of the trailing dogs. You do not want your trailing dog to smell a scent article that was contaminated after a previous trailing dog sniffed and slobbered on it before he took off on the trail; otherwise your trailing dog might focus on that first trailing dog's scent.

You also want to train extensively with other trailing dogs and set up trails using each of the trailing dogs as decoy dogs. For example, two target-dog handlers with target dogs walk straight out together, then split apart and head in opposite directions (creating a "T" formation). Work the first trailing dog on either one of those target dog scent trails. Next, bring out the second trailing dog and present him with the clean scent article from the second target dog. The second trailing dog should make the correct split in the trail and work the second target dog scent, ignoring where the first trailing dog and target dog walked.

Chapter 11
DUAL-PURPOSE
TRAINING

If you have a dog who loves to play with other dogs and also gives a physical alert of excitement when he picks up the scent of a cat, then you may have a dog who can be trained in both cat-detection and trailing work. A dog trained for both purposes is called a dual-purpose dog.

A dual-purpose dog is simply a dog who is trained as *both* a cat-detection dog used to conduct an area search for lost cats (see Chapter 9), as well as a trailing dog used to follow the scent trail of lost dogs and other animals (see Chapter 10). To train a dual purpose dog, use the exact same techniques that you used to train both the cat-detection dog and the trailing dog. Although it takes twelve to eighteen months to fully train a dual purpose dog in trailing work, the dog could be ready to work cat-detection cases within a few months.

A drawback to cross-training a search dog in two disciplines is that it has the potential for weakening the dog's search abilities. Versatility is nice, but excelling in one talent is better. Field goal kickers on football teams focus 100 percent of their efforts on kicking footballs; they don't need to practice blocking, tackling, or catching footballs. Drug dogs who are trained to find drugs and drugs alone are superior to police patrol dogs who are cross-trained to track criminals, apprehend suspects, protect their handler, conduct crowd control, search for physical evidence, *and* search for drugs. Understand that training a dog to "do it all" has limitations. If you decide to train a dual-purpose dog, realize that you have the potential of developing a dog who willingly tracks the scent trail of a lost dog, but loses concentration when he suddenly flushes a cat.

The best strategy for training a dual-purpose dog is to start with trailing work. Once you've completed trailing dog training Steps 1 through 8, then you can incorporate cat-detection training into your training program beginning with cat detection training Step 1. As you continue to train and work on trailing problems, add cat-detection training sessions every week. You use different training equipment and signals when teaching cat-detection work versus trailing work (different harness, collar, cues, and hand signals). By making a distinction between the two disciplines, the dual purpose dog learns to differentiate between detecting the airborne scent of a cat and following the aged scent trail of a dog.

How to Train
Following is an outline of how to integrate the training steps needed for a dual-purpose dog found in Chapter 9 (cat detection) and Chapter 10 (trailing dog).

Begin with trailing dog training (Chapter 10) and teach the following steps:

Step 1: "Take Scent" cue

Step 2: Short sock throw

Step 3: Short L-trail

Step 4: L-trail with sock

Step 5: Cover the eyes

Step 6: Cover the eyes II

Step 7: Hiding

Step 8: Out of view

Next, incorporate the following cat detection steps (Chapter 9) into the training program:

Step 1: "Check this"

Step 2: "This way"

Step 3: "Where?"

Step 4: Imprinting

Step 5: Crated cats

Step 6: Find and paw

Step 7: Advanced training

Decomposition training (see Chapter 12)

At any point during cat-detection training (Steps 1 through 7) you can work on trailing dog training Steps 9 through 30.

The Distinction Between Trailing and Cat Detection

To help the dual purpose dog maintain a clear distinction between the two disciplines, I suggest that you do not work cat-detection training steps on the same day that you work trailing steps. With trailing-dog training, you teach the dog to remain focused on an older, colder scent trail (of a dog) and to ignore the fresher scents that he encounters, including the scent of any cats in the area. In cat-detection work, you teach the dog to search an area, sniff in locations where you direct him to sniff, until he finds the very fresh, airborne scent of a cat, and finally finds the stationary cat.

Utilizing different equipment (collar, harness, etc.) for trailing than what you use for cat-detection work helps make a clear distinction between the two disciplines. You can place a small bell (sold for cat collars) on a special collar that you only use on the dog during cat-detection work and use a different collar with *no* bell for trailing work. You can also use one type of tracking harness for area search work and a harness that fits and feels different to the dog when trailing lost dogs.

With trailing, you ask the dog to follow a trail of scent that is on the ground or clinging to bushes or grass. You expect the dog to trot along as he follows the path of scent; with cat-detection work, the dog slowly searches, under your direction, and investigates all bushes, and nooks and crannies for the strongest source of cat scent. Although I don't discourage the use of dual-purpose dogs (I'm currently in the process of training one myself), the ideal situation is for you to train one dog who strictly trails lost dogs and a second dog who is strictly a cat-detection dog. You might even consider training a third dog in case something happens to one of your primary working dogs. However, I understand that adding yet another dog to your pack is often not feasible, so cross-training one dog in two different disciplines (cat detection and trailing in order to have a dual purpose dog) may be your only option.

Chapter 12

DECOMPOSITION
TRAINING

Although it may be unpleasant, it is important to train a MAR dog to detect the scent of animal decomposition. Whether training a dog in trailing, cat-detection, or dual-purpose work, you need a dog who will pinpoint the location of animal decomposition scent if it is anywhere in the search area. As traumatic as it is to find a deceased pet, most people would rather have closure than to remain in a constant state of grief, never knowing what happened to the missing pet.

You must accept the fact that finding deceased pets or the remains of missing pets will occur with MAR work. Every professional searcher, including search-and-rescue volunteers who track missing people, understand that there's always a possibility that the object of the search could be found deceased. If you search for lost pets, you will eventually recover a lost pet who has died. This is very difficult, but it is even more difficult to give a death notification to a pet owner who is hoping and praying the missing pet will be found alive and safe.

My search dogs have located many deceased cats. In several cases, the cats were consumed by coyotes and the only evidence that remained was clumps of fur, bone chips and in one case, a few internal organs. Because it's likely that you will find deceased pets, you need to know what your dog will do when he comes across the odor of decomposing animal scent. You learn this through decomposition training.

A DNA test confirmed that this clump of fur (recovered at a coyote kill-site) belonged to a missing cat named Cleo.

Obtaining Training Materials

You must obtain a portion of a cat or dog carcass to use as a "training aid." If you're training a cat-detection dog, train only on deceased cat scent. But if you're training a trailing dog or a dual-purpose dog, then you should train on the scent of various deceased animals: dog, cat, ferret, and reptile. Initially, start with cat and dog decomposition. You can eventually incorporate decomposing scents of other species that you might search for.

You want to have at least two different types of material: a *fresh* training aid and an *aged* training aid. An example of a fresh training aid is tissue from fresh road kill or tissues removed from spay/neuter surgeries. An example of an aged training aid is a fully decomposed deceased animal that is leathery and dried out, such as a flattened carcass of an animal who has been dead for several months. Both of these are decomposing animal tissue, but they smell different and have different levels of bacterial action.

When obtaining fresh and aged canine training aids, make sure you're positive that the deceased dog was fully vaccinated and that it did not die from a contagious canine disease. There could be a slight danger of disease transition if your dog is exposed to diseased decomposing dog material. For this reason, I suggest obtaining all deceased body parts from a veterinarian who is familiar with the health of the donor dog. With cats, it is different because very few diseases can be transmitted from a sick cat to a dog.

According to the American Veterinary Medical Association (AVMA), there are no national regulations pertaining to veterinary medical waste disposal. Instead, this is regulated on a state level. Thus depending on where you live, some veterinarians will be glad to provide you with training materials while others will not. In most cases, non-contaminated animal parts are treated as "medical solid waste" and are simply disposed as normal trash (meaning it should be easy for you to obtain these materials from a vet) whereas body parts infected with diseases are treated as a "regulated medical waste" and are considered "Biohazardous."

If you determine that your veterinarian is authorized to release non-diseased animal parts to you, then the easiest and safest way to obtain training aids is to simply leave two glass jars at the vet's office and have him/her "donate" all dog and cat gonads from neuter surgeries. Your veterinarian can refrigerate these animal parts until you are ready to stop by their practice to pick them up. However, I do not recommend using gonads from neuter surgeries of shelter dogs in which many of the "strays" have unknown health backgrounds. All animal parts should come from healthy, vaccinated animals.

I also do *not* recommend that you pick up and use a fully intact, fresh victim of "road kill" you happen to find on the side of the road. Not only is the health of such an animal unknown, but removing the remains could mean you'd deny someone closure of a beloved family pet who's missing. Deceased dogs and cats like this should be reported to animal control.

Store the training aids inside small jars (baby food) that you can keep within a second, larger jar (mayonnaise) as this will help slow down the rate of decomposition. You can even use a third container, such a metal ammunition box, to store the jars. Thus, you provide three barriers to slow down the rate of decomposition and reduce the chances of maggot infestation. You need two lids for each small jar. One (intact) lid is used to store the training aid. The second lid is ventilated with several holes and used during training so the decomposition scent can escape from the jar, but flies can't get into the jar. Use a hammer and a nail and puncture the training lid several times, making sure the holes you create are too small for a fly to enter.

Store decomposition material inside a small jar kept within a larger jar.

Another option is to create a plastic "scent tube" training aid made out of PVC pipe. You can create scent tubes by cutting PVC pipe into eight-inch pieces. Drill several holes about the size of a fingernail on either side the entire length of the tube. Get two PVC pipe caps for each tube, one that you can cement in place and the other that you can remove to insert decomposition material. Place the animal decomposition material inside a knee-high nylon (secured with a knot on the end) and then stuff the nylon into the scent tube. A third storage option is to use wire mesh cricket tubes sold as fishing tackle at most sporting goods stores. You can store your animal decomposition tubes inside a large glass pickle or mayonnaise jar.

Most cadaver-dog handlers keep cadaver samples in a freezer (usually one that is *not* used to store food). However, freezing decomposition training aids has limitations. You need to let the training aid thaw out before you use it. Freezing and thawing material inhibits the formation of bacteria that forms during natural decomposition. Tissue that decomposes at room temperature is closer to the odor that the dog will detect during a lost-pet investigation than tissue that decomposes slowly through repetitive freezing and thawing. You can learn more about storing decomposition materials by reading articles about how cadaver dog handlers store human cadaver materials. (A great source of information on storing cadaver materials can be found at www.cadaverdog.com.)

You will train the dog to detect the scent of animal decomposition in five simple steps:

1. Imprint on decomposition scent

2. "Push" jar

3. Find jar, "Push" jar

4. Find and paw at inaccessible jar

5. Find material and "Dig-dig"

Step 1: Imprint on Decomposition Scent

To imprint the dog to the odor of decomposition, you simply introduce him to the scent of cat or dog decomposition while using a decomposition cue. This teaches him to associate the cue word with the decomposition scent. Reminder: Because the pet owner searches along with you most of the time, select a decomposition cue that is not plainly understood as "dead pet scent." Do not use cues like "Bones" or "Find dead." Bill Tolhurst, a legendary Bloodhound trainer, suggested using the word "Na-poo," which is the Indian word for dead. I personally prefer the word, "Comp," an abbreviated version of the word decomposition.

Be sure to wear rubber gloves when handling training aids. Place the training aid (baby jar, wire cricket tube, or PVC scent tube) in a concealed, but secure location, such as tall grass or bushes where it won't be disturbed by people or animals. Allow it to remain in one location for more than one hour, giving time for a scent pool to form around the aid.

Harness the dog as you normally do before working a search problem. Give him the "Search!" cue and allow him to search around while heading toward the training aid. As you approach the decomposition scent, watch the dog for a reaction.

Ideally, you will notice a moderate to strong level of interest, perhaps rapid sniffing or a head jerk, when he picks up the decomposition scent. Immediately, when you notice the dog react to the scent, say the decomposition cue ("Comp") so that he learns to associate the word with the decomposition scent. Praise him and use the "Wheerrree?" encouragement cue so that he focuses on the scent. Allow the dog to find the training aid, praising him all the while. While the dog is at the jar or tube, continue to repeat the decomposition cue while praising and rewarding him with a treat. You should repeat this imprinting work twice a day for a week

The dog should show interest in the decomposition odor.

Step 2: "Push" Jar

Now that the dog has been exposed to the scent of decomposition, you need to incorporate the "Push" cue (covered in Chapter 9) and teach him to push on the training aid that contains the odor of decomposition. Initially, you start the session by working only on the push without bringing in the decomposition element. With the dog in harness and the training aid nearby, ask the dog to sit and give him the "Push" cue. Click and treat when he pushes on your outstretched hand (repeat this exercise five times).

Next, set the training aid (decomposition material inside a baby jar or tube) on the ground in front of the dog. Place your other hand, palm up, directly on top of the training aid and give the "Push!" cue. When the dog pushes on your hand (which you should hold just above the training aid) click and treat. Repeat this five times.

When the dog pushes on your hand, click and treat.

Next, pick up the training aid and hold it in one hand directly in front of the dog. Give him the "Push!" cue. Make sure that his paw hits the training aid when he pushes at your hand (that's holding the training aid). Get the dog used to pushing and hitting the training aid. Click and treat only when his paw touches the training aid. Be sure that every time he touches the training aid, you click and treat. He learns quickly that every time he paws at (and touches) the scent jar, he is rewarded.

Step 3: Find Jar, "Push" Jar

By now the dog is imprinted on decomposition scent and is interested in finding it. He is also trained to push on a container (jar or tube) that contains decomposition scent. Your next step is to hide the training aid, give him the "Search!" cue, and he searches the area for the hidden aid. As he picks up the scent and alerts, ask him, "Where's the comp?" When he finds the jar, give him the "Push" cue. Once he pushes on the aid (which is on the ground), click and treat, and praise him.

Click-and-treat once the dog pushes on the training aid that is on the ground.

Repeat this step twice in one training session for about a week. Once the dog finds the training aid, pause in silence to see if he pushes on it without you giving the cue. If the dog is clicker savvy, he will probably realize that he can trigger the click and treat if he pushes on the jar or tube. Immediately click, treat, and praise when he pushes on the training aid on his own.

Step 4: Find and Paw at Inaccessible Jar

By now the dog is accustomed to searching an area to find a concealed cat, a concealed dog, and/or a concealed jar (or tube) of animal decomposition scent. Now he needs to learn what to do when he finds decomposition scent that is concealed, but inaccessible. You want to teach him to paw at decomposition scent he can't access. This is critical because if during an investigation your search dog encounters the odor of decomposition in a shed, for example, he should focus on the scent and paw at the shed door to indicate to you he's found the source.

To teach the dog to paw at inaccessible decomposition, hide the material and leave it unattended for at least a day. If you use a baby jar, be sure to use the lid with holes punched in it so the scent can escape. Hide the jar (or tube) inside a shed (right by the door) or under a house right next to a crawl space screen. After a day has passed, walk the dog through the area, asking him to "Check this" at various areas before you lead him up to the shed door (or screen) and give the same "Check this" cue. When the dog alerts, probably with intensive sniffing, encourage him, but wait for him to paw at the shed door or the screen on his own. If he doesn't paw on his own, give the "Push" cue and praise him when he paws at the door or screen. You can also use the "Comp" cue once you know he smells the decomposition scent. Once you bring out the training aid, praise the dog and give him treats. Through repeated training exercises, the dog will learn to paw when there's a large scent pool of animal decomposition.

Step 5: Find Material and "Dig-dig"

In addition to teaching the dog to paw at the inaccessible source of decomposition scent, you also need to teach him to dig with both paws (or just scratch with one paw) at the odor of decomposition scent that has seeped into dirt or asphalt.

You have already taught the dog the "Dig-dig" cue by using food (hot dog) scent (see Chapter 8). But instead of using pieces of hot dog in a baby jar, put animal decomposition material in the jar. Place the jar down into a hole in the ground and give the "Dig-dig" cue. Alternate the "Comp" cue with the "Dig-dig" cue as the dog digs at the jar. Both of these cues are familiar to the dog so it should be easy for him to learn to dig with both paws at the decomposition scent. If you're using a clicker, click and treat as soon as he paws at the jar.

Once the dog routinely scratches or paws at the buried training aid, take him to an area where decomposition scent has seeped into the ground and give him the "Dig-dig" cue. You can train by going out to a location where the body of a cat or dog has decomposed for weeks into the soil or pavement, but the remains have been removed. Probably the best way to find locations like this would be to ask your local animal control agency or even the highway department responsible for picking up deceased animals. Explain what you are doing and ask if they could call you the next time they are called out to pick up a dead animal. Chemicals that seep from a decomposing carcass change the soil composition and are detectable to a dog long after they are invisible to a human. Cadaver dogs have been known to detect the scent of decomposition years after a body has decomposed.

Train on asphalt where an animal has decomposed leaving only a stain on the ground.

If your veterinarian agrees to release disease-free animal waste to you, then you should also ask if they would provide you with animal blood for training purposes. You can either collect it as liquid in a jar or you can have it swabbed onto sterile gauze pads. The bloody gauze pads can be placed inside a small jar for easy storage and training use. Use the same cue and imprinting method you use in other decomposition training. Dogs and cats who are struck by cars will often leave a stain of blood or scraped tissue on the pavement. Thus, your dog will need to alert to the scent of blood, tissue or bone on the asphalt should you locate a suspicious stain during a search. If your dog does alert to a stain, then you can move forward with forensic testing, such as presumptive blood analysis testing to determine if it is human or animal blood, followed by DNA testing to confirm the source of the stain. (Animal evidence collection procedures are covered in Missing Pet Partnership's MAR Technician Course.)

I probably should point out that although it is nice to train your dog to "push" (scratch with just one paw) at the source of inaccessible decomposition scent and also to "Dig-dig" (dig the ground with both paws) on the source of decomposition scent that has soaked into the ground, you can get by with training him to exhibit just one of these behaviors. It really doesn't matter if he uses one or two paws to tell you that he's found something that's dead. What matters is that the dog consistently uses his paws (to scratch or dig) at the odor of animal decomposition and that you can read his body language. If you have difficulty teaching either the "Push" or the "Dig-dig" cues, you can elect to train only one of these indicators. Use what works for your dog and stick with it.

During actual searches, you give the decomposition cue under four different circumstances. First, when you've found a stain on the ground or asphalt that you suspect could be blood and you want your dog to tell you whether or not it is animal decomposition. Second, you might need to follow up on a witness report of "dead cat in the road," but there's no carcass so you want your dog to check the area for any decomposition stains on the ground. Third, if while on a search you encounter flies (sign of possible decomposition) or you yourself catch a whiff of decomposition scent, you can ask your dog, "Comp, wheerreee?" to see if he detects the scent and can pinpoint it. Finally, if your dog makes a partial decomposition find, such as a single bone or clumps of bloody fur (indication of predator killing an animal) during the search, you can give the decomposition cue and use the dog to search for even more evidence.

One final suggestion with decomposition training is that you also train your dog to locate decomposition that is submerged under water. Although I personally have not worked cases like this, other MAR Technicians have tracked lost dogs only to have the scent trail end at a pond or a lake where the missing dog drowned.

You can train for water recovery by placing your training aid in water (a lake or pond) and weighing it down below the surface. Make sure that you either have an assistant who knows right where the training aid is anchored or that you mark the shoreline in some manner. Practice from a dock, from shore, and while wading your dog into chest deep water. If your dog can't push or dig-dig because he's inside the water, then encourage him to give a different indication (barking, whining) when the scent source is submerged.

Chapter 13
HOW TO BECOME A "PET DETECTIVE"

I use the term "pet detective" in this chapter since it is familiar to the public, and in marketing your services you may find using the term advantageous. Technically, however, I am referring to a trained MAR technician who works with certified MAR dogs (cat detection, trailing, or dual purpose), although at this point anyone can say they are a "pet detective."

Can I Making a Living?

I'm often asked whether or not a person can earn a living as a pet detective. The answer is rather complex. There is clearly a need for lost-pet services, and there are plenty of potential clients. The American Pet Products Manufactures Association estimates that in 2007 there were approximately 88.3 million cats, 74.8 million dogs, 16 million birds, 13.4 million reptiles, and 24.3 million small animals owned by families across the United States. It also estimated that pet owners spent over $40 billion on their pets during that year.

HomeAgain, a national microchip company, estimates that one out of three pets will become lost in its lifetime, and more than 10 million pets are lost or stolen every year. In spite of these numbers, the pet detective industry is only in the infant stages of development. It's difficult to predict how much of a demand there will be for lost-pet services, and much of this depends on how well the concept is promoted and accepted by the public. Factors that determine the demand for these services in your own community include the population density; the cost of living; fees; whether or not you (and your dog) are certified; your success rate; respect from local pet industry officials (veterinarians, shelter workers, etc.); and how effective you are at marketing your services.

It's safe to say that to start out you can expect to make MAR work a part-time business or as a means to supplement your current income. Profits vary depending upon your services, where you live, and whether or not you are willing to travel to conduct searches. Pet detective fees currently range anywhere from $400 per search to more than $2,000 per search.

The handful of pet detectives who are willing to travel to other parts of the country rightfully charge for travel expenses (hotel, gas, food, time, airfare, etc.). The problem is that hiring a pet detective who has to fly across the country typically requires the last-minute purchase of an airline ticket, which can cost more than $1000. Even if the pet detective drives (several days of travel expenses), the fee for services is very expensive. I have no doubt that as more pet detectives and MAR dogs are trained and certified, the law of supply and demand will dictate: service fees will drop and local demand for MAR services will increase. While the law of supply states that the higher the price ($2,000), the more the producer will supply, the law of demand states that the lower the price ($400), the more the consumer will demand it. This means that ultimately pet detectives will likely be so busy working cases in their own communities that they won't need to travel great distances to earn a living.

Until there's a strong demand for MAR services in your community, you are better off offering your services as a side business. Many professionals in the pet industry have already added MAR services to their existing pet sitting, dog training, and dog daycare businesses, and don't rely on pet detective fees as a sole source of income. We've already seen veterinarians interested in launching lost-pet services through their practices, and a few veterinary technicians who plan to "moonlight" as pet detectives to supplement their incomes. If the demand for lost-pet services continues to increase (just as the demand for pet sitters, dog walkers, and dog daycare centers has increased), it's likely that within the next ten years there will be veterinary clinics, dog daycare centers, and even animal shelters that employ full-time pet detectives. Thankfully, this means that fee-based, lost-pet services will ultimately be affordable and widely available.

MAR Technician Certification

Imagine a police dog trained to apprehend criminals partnered with a civilian who doesn't know how to affect an arrest. Or imagine a search-and-rescue dog trained to locate victims of a terrorist attack in a collapsed building partnered with someone who doesn't know the first thing about how to navigate safely within a collapsed structure. This book only teaches you how to train a MAR dog. Missing Pet Partnership, however, offers Missing Animal Response Technician certification courses that teach *you* the science of *how, when,* and *where* to search for lost pets.

MAR technicians who attend this training learn how to solve lost-pet investigations using the same law enforcement-based investigative techniques used to solve lost-person investigations. This includes the use of CSI-type techniques, such as the application of deductive reasoning, search probability theory, deception detection, behavioral profiling to predict distances that lost pets travel, and the use of high-tech equipment (search cameras, amplified listening devices, and humane traps with baby monitors). In addition, MAR technicians are trained in how to collect and analyze physical evidence, how to use DNA testing and forensic anthropologists to solve cases, how to use presumptive blood testing to analyze suspected kill sites, and how to identify wildlife tracks and scat (i.e., coyote droppings, owl pellets, etc.).

MAR technicians learn how, when, and where to search for lost pets.

Topics that are covered in the MAR technician course include:

- How and when to use high-tech equipment versus trained search dogs to find lost pets.

- How pets behave when lost, how far they travel, and the most probable locations where they can be found.

- How behavior (human and animal) influences the chances that a lost dog or lost cat will be reunited with an owner.

- How to use "trap-and-reunite" and "attract-and-capture" techniques to recover panicked dogs and cats (i.e. after natural disasters or fireworks on New Year's Eve and July 4th).

- How to use deductive reasoning to process clues, search probability theory to know where to search, and behavioral profiling to predict the distance a lost pet will travel.

- How to use presumptive blood analysis, DNA testing, scatology, and forensic anthropology to solve lost pet investigations.

- How to offer MAR services in your community as a side business, as a new service through an existing business, or as a community service through a nonprofit organization

MPP recently revised the MAR Technician course so that students can now bring their dogs to our seminar for evaluations and preliminary training. In some cases our course includes the additional option where

MAR technicians are trained to use presumptive blood test kits to analyze suspected blood stains.

students can respond on actual lost pet investigations with a certified MAR dog and receive practical field experience. We've also created additional training for MAR Technicians through our new Wilderness MAR Technician course. MAR Technicians spend five days learning technical skills like wilderness survival, awareness, bird language, and animal tracking.

As a word of warning, be careful of "poser" pet detectives promoting services or training programs that lack the experience and knowledge that we have at MPP. We recently discovered a group who had cut and paste text directly from our web site in order to promote a pet detective training program and business that does not even exist! Just because you see pet detectives in the media or find a web site that looks or sounds impressive does not mean they are legitimate. For more information and a schedule of our MAR seminars, visit www.missingpetpartnership.com.

MAR Dog Certification

Certification is simply the process of proving capabilities through unbiased testing offered through an impartial evaluator. With traditional search-and-rescue dogs, police patrol dogs, drug-detection dogs, and bomb dogs, a standardized test is administered by a local, statewide, or national organization or government entity that does not have a vested interest in the outcome of the test. In other words, the evaluator is impartial and does not stand to profit if the dog passes the examination. Missing Pet Partnership offers evaluation, training, and certification services for MAR technicians willing to travel (with their dogs) to various locations across the United States to attend our seminars.

In addition, I've listed MAR dog trainers in the Resources that I recommend for lessons, training consultations, and for administering Missing Pet Partnership's MAR cat-detection and trailing dog tests. If you live anywhere near any of these individuals, I strongly suggest you contact them and consider training with them. It is vital that you receive professional feedback from experienced trainers who can guide you in training. Once your dog is advanced in training, you really need to meet with a trustworthy trainer who can set up blind trails for you to work. This helps you gauge if you are ready for certification. Obviously, the few people I've listed cannot test and certify dogs from all over the nation but, thankfully, this list of trainers will only continue to grow.

Volunteer vs. Paid Pet Detectives

There will always be a need for both for-profit pet detectives and volunteer pet detectives. Here's a breakdown for the benefits, the drawbacks, the needs, and the opportunities for both volunteer and paid pet detectives.

Volunteer Pet Detectives

Volunteer pet detectives are people who donate their time through an established nonprofit organization (animal shelter, rescue group, animal welfare organization, or animal disaster response team). Nonprofits typically charge a nominal fee for services rendered or they simply accept a donation in any amount for services. If the family can't afford to pay, a nonprofit organization has the freedom to offer assistance without expecting payment.

Benefits. The plus to local, volunteer pet detectives is that there is always more volunteers available in any given community than there will be full-time paid pet detectives. Many services that are too time consuming (and too expensive to hire a full time pet detective) can be accomplished by volunteers. This includes services such as checking shelters, intersection alerts, neighborhood checks, and trap-and-reunite surveillance work. Volunteers can also respond and assist to recover lost pets in disaster situations where charging a fee for lost-pet services, especially when someone has lost everything he owns, would be unethical.

Drawbacks. More often than not, volunteers are not immediately available to respond to searches whereas, depending on how far away they live, for-profit pet detectives can drop what they're doing and respond right away. Volunteers are only used occasionally, thus their level of experience might not be as high as a full-time pet detective.

Need. There is always a need for volunteers! Whether the incident is a natural or man-made disaster or simply a case of a local lost pet, volunteers who can help on a local and national level in any manner are needed. Pet owners should not be alone in their efforts to find a lost pet and should have some type of assistance available if they cannot afford to hire a pet detective.

Opportunities. Missing Pet Partnership has developed a Lost Pet First Responder Network consisting of MAR-trained volunteers who'd like to offer hands-on assistance should a pet become lost in their own community. Volunteering for this network could be as simple as conducting a shelter check, using a trained MAR dog, conducting an intersection alert, posting florescent posters, or assisting in humanely trapping a displaced cat or panicked dog. Volunteers in this program receive 20-hours of instruction through Missing Pet Partnership's MAR First Responder seminar. For a listing of upcoming MAR First Responder seminars, visit www.missingpetpartnership.org. In addition, HomeAgain®, a national microchip company, recently launched a new "PetRescuers" program which includes a national network of volunteers willing to receive lost pet e-mail alerts when a pet becomes lost in their community.

Paid Pet Detectives

Benefits. The plus to for-profit pet detectives is that they're often able to respond immediately; volunteers can be limited because they may be unable to leave their paying jobs to respond to searches. For-profit pet detectives are able to work more cases than volunteers, thus increasing their on-the-job experience and success rate. Best of all, for-profit pet detectives are paid for their passion of working with dogs and helping people and animals in need.

Drawbacks. Currently, unless you live in a large city, there probably isn't enough of a demand for lost-pet services to sustain a small, local pet detective business. Becoming a full-time pet detective at this point in time requires travel with fees that are often too high for most pet owners, making these services available only to the elite who can afford it. Plus, if you've never owned and operated a business, it can be quite a challenge to launch into a career that requires that you market your services, maintain a set of books, and manage a small business.

Need. There is always a need for paid pet detectives with qualified search dogs. With millions of pets lost every year, there should eventually be enough business to sustain for-profit pet detectives who want to make a living in this new industry. The fly in the ointment is that the process of obtaining credibility and the trust of the pet-owning public is going to take time. But, as the demand for lost-pet services and the national marketing of MAR services increases, your chances of being able to operate your own business or to find employment within this industry is likely to increase.

Opportunities. Missing Pet Partnership currently markets for-profit MAR technicians who have graduated from our training program through our web site at www.missingpetpartnership.org. The national credibility and marketing power of Missing Pet Partnership, including our plans to develop national standards, a code of ethics, and ultimately an international association of pet detectives, positions our organization as the perfect place to obtain your training, certification, and to market your services.

Missing Pet Partnership

Although this book gives you the tools to help you train your dog to locate lost pets, eventually there will be a source where you can obtain a MAR dog who is already trained. Missing Pet Partnership plans to build a national training center (near Seattle, WA) that will facilitate the proper training and certification of MAR dogs. Once funded and staffed, MPP will pull unwanted dogs from shelters (dogs who have passed our evaluation), train them, certify them, and lease them to partnering veterinarians, shelters, rescue groups, and individual pet detectives. Like service dog organizations that house, train, and distribute guide dogs and assistance dogs, Missing Pet Partnership hopes to be a leading supplier of MAR dogs within the pet detective community. Please consider supporting our efforts to train and certify MAR dogs by making a tax-deductible contribution to Missing Pet Partnership, P.O. Box 2457, Clovis, CA 93613. If you'd like to read more about our development, lost-pet recovery stories, and training opportunities you can sign up to receive our Scent Detectives quarterly newsletter by going to www.missingpetpartnership.org.

Realities of MAR Work

Having a MAR dog does not mean that you'll find every lost pet. In some investigations, the key to getting a pet back could be as simple as posting a florescent lost-pet poster. Just recently, a woman called me because her yellow Labrador Retriever puppy had dug out of the yard and was lost. I was heading out to a meeting and I didn't have time to respond with my Bloodhound, Chase. But I quickly created a giant, bright orange "Reward—Lost Dog" poster with her work and home phone numbers. I took a roll of duct tape and posted two of these signs at a major intersection near her home (which happened to be on the way to my meeting). This took only fifteen (volunteer) minutes of my time. I came home five hours later to a phone message that informed me that Pismo, the yellow Lab puppy, was home because the person who had found him saw the poster. Without much effort, simple acts like this can generate appreciation (and donors) for your nonprofit organization, testimonials for your business marketing materials, and referrals to future paying clients.

Pet detective work is physically demanding. You should be in good physical shape if you plan to jog behind a trailing dog, navigate rough terrain, or crawl under houses as you search for a lost cat.

Pet detective work is inconvenient. Once friends, family, neighbors, and your community learn that you're a pet detective, you'll be called on weekends, holidays, while on vacation, and at all hours and asked to immediately respond to help search for a lost pet.

Pet detective work is quirky. You'll be laughed at, treated like you're a nut, and worshipped like a hero all in the same week!!!

Pet detective work is stressful. There is a lot of pressure to help grieving, panic-stricken people who see you as a savior.

Pet detective work can lead to burn out. It won't take long before the pressure of being the only person in your community who is able to offer this service will wear on you. Compassion fatigue—the point where you become burned out and tired of helping grieving, needy people—can set in.

Pet detective work is heartbreaking. You may find more deceased pets and have cases with no closure than cases with happy, textbook reunions.

Pet detective work is exciting, unpredictable, and fascinating. It is police work mixed with animal rescue work. If you love both forensics and animals, then Missing Animal Response might just be the right work for you!

If you love forensic work and animals, MAR work might be the right vocation for you.

Chapter 14
CASE STUDIES

Perhaps the best way to motivate you to get out and train your dog is to share some of my more interesting and instructive cases. Some have happy endings and some have sad endings, but you can learn something from each. Work hard with your dog and, eventually, you will have your own collection of lost-pet recovery stories!

Lost Dogs

Tai
Trailing dog establishes direction of travel

Tai's owner watched in horror as his Akita, Tai, was hit by a car after chasing a cat. When Tai took off running in a blind panic, his owner immediately chased after him. He last saw Tai head east into the woods on the east side of Highway 9, a two-lane road that snakes through the Santa Cruz Mountains in Northern California. Tai's owner searched the woods until late that night before he called me. I responded the following morning with my search dog, Rachel. By the time I arrived, Tai had been missing for sixteen hours and it was raining. I scented Rachel on Tai's bedding. Rachel picked up a scent trail and headed north, then cut east into the woods where Tai was last seen.

Rachel circled and worked this area of the woods for about fifteen minutes. This was our target area since it was the point last seen. If Tai was severely injured, he probably crawled into or under something rather than continue to run. To my surprise, Rachel worked out of the woods back onto Highway 9, headed west crossing over the highway, climbed up a steep embankment and turned north along a set of railroad tracks. Because I was working a trailing dog and was at the mercy of trusting her nose, I did not interfere with where she led me.

Rachel trailed along the railroad tracks for almost two miles until we reached a train trestle. Rachel did not show interest in crossing the trestle and Tai's owner told me that Tai would never cross such a dangerous path. We did a quick check of the area, but did not find Tai. Because I was short on time (I had to go to work), I terminated our trailing work. I instructed Tai's owner to search the wooded area on the west side of the train tracks since Rachel had indicated that Tai had run north along the tracks.

Tai's owner called me three hours later saying that he had walked along the tracks in the area near the trestle, calling for Tai when Tai came from out of the woods on the west side of the tracks! Even though she did not track right up to Tai, Rachel's trailing work led Tai's owner to focus his search on the opposite side of the highway, a factor that was instrumental in Tai's recovery.

Coco
Trailing dog confirms direction of travel and sighting

Coco, a seventeen-year-old blind and deaf Chihuahua mix, wandered out an open gate at her home in San Jose, California. Coco was wearing a collar with identification tags. She was a treasured member of a family of two devastated people who had raised Coco since she was a tiny puppy.

I responded with Rachel four days later. Using Coco's dog dish as a scent article, Rachel picked up a scent trail heading west along a residential street. Rachel then turned south, working for three blocks and then turned west along another small residential street. Shortly after making this turn, Rachel lost the scent.

I mapped out the trail where Rachel had worked the scent and gave the information to Coco's owners. I instructed Coco's owners to go door-to-door with flyers to all of the homes along the route that Rachel had led us in hopes of finding someone who had seen Coco or perhaps had picked her up.

That evening, Coco's owners went door to door as instructed. They discovered a witness (at a house along the route Rachel trailed) who said he found Coco in his side yard the evening Coco disappeared. The man shooed Coco out of his yard because he did not realize the dog was a blind, lost pet. In his mind, Coco was just someone's wandering dog snooping around in his yard. This is a form of "rescuer behavior" that is covered in Missing Pet Partnership's MAR Technician Course. What this man (a potential rescuer who came into contact with Coco) believed about Coco (that she was simply a stray dog) influenced how he behaved.

The local news media filmed Rachel working this search and created a "lost Coco" story that ran in the evening news. It is a rare opportunity for a pet owner to get media attention for a lost pet. However, in spite of the news coverage, no one ever returned Coco, no new leads were developed, and Coco was never found.

George
Injured dog found by establishing direction of travel

George, a three-year-old Airedale, escaped from a fenced pasture and was missing in Hollister, California. His owner, Bob, did not know which direction George had taken or where he could possibly be. I responded forty-five hours after George's disappearance.

Using George's sheepskin bedding as scent material, Rachel picked up a scent trail near a busy roadway, tracked south and then west into an orchard where she lost the scent. Because my Bloodhound, A.J., was experiencing health problems, I used my Bloodhound, Chase, instead. Chase picked up the same scent trail as Rachel, but worked it differently. Chase trailed further south, cut west and deep into the orchard, and eventually lost the scent.

I instructed Bob to focus his search for George south of his location and to search the orchards. Immediately after I left, Bob climbed into his truck and drove a mile south and turned west on the first road he came to. Bob looked to his left and spotted George sitting in the center of a field. George was immobile because he had been hit by a car. Although he was dehydrated, in shock, and had a severely broken leg that required surgery, George survived and went on to become active in agility and other dog sports!

Tika
Trailing dogs establish direction of travel

Tika, a four-year-old Pomeranian, escaped out the front door of her family's apartment on a cold, January evening in Los Gatos, California. Her owner had just returned from a trip and Tika slipped by unnoticed into the dark while luggage was carried into the house. An hour later, the owner discovered Tika was missing.

I responded the following afternoon with search dogs, Rachel and Chase. Using two sterile gauze pads, I collected Tika's scent from her blanket. I presented one of the gauze pads to Rachel who picked up a trail that went south through the apartment complex, turned around and worked north and then east into a used car parking lot where she lost the trail.

I loaded Rachel into the truck and returned to the apartment with my Bloodhound, Chase. Using the second gauze pad, I presented it to Chase who picked up a trail that headed east. Chase did not work the area south into the complex like Rachel had worked, but she worked east along the sidewalk over into the same used car parking lot. Chase then worked up to the sidewalk of the busy six-lane roadway (which the apartment faced) for a block east of the apartment and lost the scent directly across the street from a Starbucks. Due to the danger of traffic, I did not allow Chase to cross the street. We terminated our search at this point, convinced that the trail ended at the used car lot and that someone had picked Tika up at that point.

I instructed Tika's owner to place florescent "Reward—Lost Dog" posters along the roadway, which she did the next day. The day after that, she called me. The person who picked Tika up the evening she escaped spotted the poster. He found Tika at the Starbucks directly across from where Chase lost the scent trail. In retrospect, I should have waited for traffic to clear and taken Chase across the street to see if the scent trail continued on the other side (refer to the "Daisy" search in which this technique paid off).

Daisy
Trailing dog establishes direction of travel

Daisy, a one-year-old Rotweiller, pulled out of her collar and escaped from her foster handler's care in a busy area of Fresno, California. Daisy had just been rescued from a no-kill shelter after being neglected by her first owner. She had an extremely fearful temperament and panicked when taken out of her foster handler's car. Daisy backed out of her collar and bolted north along a four-lane, busy roadway. Her foster handler chased behind, but lost sight of Daisy when she turned east along a major six-lane roadway. By the time the foster handler rounded the corner, Daisy was nowhere in sight.

The foster hander is a friend of mine who called me immediately. I responded with my Bloodhound, Chase, and arrived within an hour of the escape. Using Daisy's collar, I scented Chase at the point last seen: on the sidewalk at the southeast corner of the intersection. Chase picked up a trail heading east, working along the sidewalk. On at least two occasions, she dipped into an office complex, but then worked her way back out along the sidewalk. After working along the sidewalk for over a block and near a side street that headed south, Chase lost the scent trail.

I allowed Chase to check south on the side street, but she turned around and shook off, which indicated that the scent did not head that way. I took her back to the sidewalk farther east, but she showed no interest and indicated there was no scent farther east. I took her back onto the side street and walked her south for half a block, checking both sides, but Chase did not pick up a scent trail and showed no interest.

I was perplexed. The area west was not an option because Daisy was a panicked dog who bolted—she would not turn around and head back in the direction she came from. The area east made sense because it was the same route she had taken with no obstructions, but Chase indicated the scent did not go any farther east. The area north was a six-lane roadway (Shaw Avenue) congested with a lot of traffic; it was a Friday at 5:00 p.m. when the escape took place. I did not see any skid marks in the roadway, and it just didn't seem as though Daisy would run into traffic when she could run south instead. The street south led into a quiet neighborhood, an area that made sense for a dog to run to, but Chase had no interest in that area.

I decided to trust my dog and believed there was no Daisy scent south or east, and that Daisy must have turned north and crossed the six-lane road. Directly across the street from that side street that headed south (and from where Chase lost the scent) was a small roadway that led into a massive apartment complex. Due to darkness and the busy traffic, we decided not to jaywalk. I walked Chase east to the next major intersection, crossed north, turned west along the north side of the highway and headed toward the entrance of the apartment complex.

As soon as we approached the grass in front of the apartment complex, Chase lunged into the harness and nearly pulled me off my feet! She began dragging me north through the complex, a confirmation that there was Daisy scent in that area. We hit a dead end in the complex, which was fenced, and eventually lost the scent. I could not figure out if someone in the complex had rescued Daisy or where Chase had missed a turn.

I convinced the foster handler to post the giant lost-dog posters (you can see samples of how to make these at www.missingpetpartnership.org). It started to rain and she was heartbroken, convinced that her efforts to help this dog had likely caused the dog to be killed. In spite of feeling hopeless, the foster handler went ahead and created the florescent posters that night and posted them the next day.

As she was taping up one of the posters, someone came up to the foster handler and told her they had just seen a black dog in a field on a street just north of there. The foster handler rushed over there and found Daisy huddled in a vacant field directly behind the apartment complex where Chase had lost the scent. After a brief chase and much effort, the foster handler was able to corner Daisy by a fence, capture her, and take her home. Daisy was later adopted by another friend of mine who spoils her like all dogs deserve to be spoiled!

Ren
Trailing dog identifies end of scent trail

Six-year-old Ren, a Chihuahua mix, dug out from his yard in San Jose, California, and was missing in an urban, residential neighborhood. Three days after he was missing, Ren's owner called for help. Unfortunately, I was not available. Instead I dispatched Jo Danehy and her newly trained MAR trailing dog, Kelsey, a Golden Retriever trained in scent discrimination trailing. Jo scented Kelsey on Ren's bedding. As a family member followed on a bicycle, Kelsey picked up a scent trail that led from the family's home to a park nearby. Kelsey lost the scent at the park. Since there had been no recent sightings of Ren, it was theorized that someone had picked up Ren at the park.

The following day, I responded with my Bloodhound, Chase. I scented Chase on Ren's collar (which came off when Ren squirmed under the fence) and Chase immediately picked up a scent trail. According to the family member who had watched Kelsey work the trail, Chase worked a similar trail that Kelsey worked, but not the exact same trail. This assured us that Chase was following Ren's scent and not Kelsey's scent. Chase ended up at the same park as Kelsey. Chase circled the park, but would not leave it. We did a perimeter check of the surrounding areas to see if Chase would pick up a scent trail leaving the park, but she did not.

I debriefed the owner and explained that based on the scent work of both trailing dogs, it appeared that Ren had ended up at the park and someone had probably removed him from the park. I instructed Ren's owner to distribute missing pet flyers within the park in both English and Spanish.

The following day, Ren's owner called with exciting news. Someone saw her flyer at the park and had found Ren. Ren was rescued the same day he disappeared at the same park that both Kelsey and Chase had trailed to.

There is no bigger thrill for a dog handler than to get one of these phone calls after you work your search dog on a case: "Guess what? Your dog was right!"

Sheila
Trailing dog establishes direction of travel

Sheila, a nine-year-old Australian Shepherd, dug under a fence and escaped in fear when neighbor kids set off firecrackers in central Fresno, California. I responded the following morning, fifteen hours after the escape, with trailing dog, Chase. There had been no sightings and Sheila's owner had no idea which direction she had traveled.

I scented Chase on Shelia's bedding and she picked up a trail heading east from Sheila's home. Chase worked along the sidewalk next to a small residential road until we came to the first intersection. Chase worked into the intersection and east, but lost the scent trail. I brought her back to the west side of the street and Chase picked up a trail heading south. She continued crossing over two small streets, worked just past the third street and lost the scent. Chase turned herself around and picked up the scent heading west along that third street, heading straight toward a major roadway (Palm Avenue).

When we worked up to the major roadway, I stopped Chase and took her by the collar (a signal that we were simply taking a break). I checked for skid marks, but did not find any. I was skeptical about the trail Chase had worked because it did not seem possible that Shelia could have successfully crossed a busy four-lane roadway without being hit by a car.

When the traffic was clear, we jogged across to the other side of the street. I told Chase to get back to work (continuing west) while on that same road, but she led me about three house lengths onto the street, turned around, shook off, and indicated there was no scent there. I allowed her to check the street north and south, but she did not pick up a scent trail on either side of the street. I terminated our search.

Several hours later, Sheila's owner called. Sheila was back home. Although her owner could not verify the exact path that Sheila had taken, at the time we worked the scent trail, Sheila was inside a house (or maybe in a yard) directly north of where Chase lost the scent trail. We had missed the turn, but Chase led us across Palm Avenue and to within one house of finding Sheila.

As it turns out, the man who found Sheila was working in his garage the evening before when Sheila ran inside. She was clearly panicked. The man closed the garage, felt sorry for Sheila, and actually planned to keep her because she was so sweet and afraid. He told his brother about the dog. The next day, the man's brother called and told him that Sheila belonged to a well-known talk radio host who had put out a plea for Sheila, his daughter's lost dog. When the man realized that Sheila belonged to someone well-known, he called the radio station and Sheila was home within an hour.

Lost Cats

Patio
Outdoor-access cat recovered near cadaver alert

Patio, a 4-year-old outdoor-access gray tabby cat just vanished from home. I used Rachel to conduct an area search (cat-detection mode) of the owner's property and the neighbor's homes within Patio's territory. During our search, Rachel located a deceased cat in the creek behind the owner's home. The deceased cat was identified as a neighbor's fourteen-year-old cat, Miss Charles, who had been missing for twelve days.

Rachel showed intense interest underneath the deck attached to Patios's home. But because of Rachel's size and the limited space underneath the deck, Rachel was not able to search that area. I noticed a two-foot opening at the base of the house (directly under the front deck), but I could not access it because the deck above it was too low. I pointed out the opening to the owner as a potential hiding spot, especially since Rachel showed interest under the deck. At this point I concluded my investigation.

Eight days later, Patio's owner contacted us to say that she had found Patio. She had detected the odor of decomposition while standing on her front porch. Recalling the crawl space that I had pointed out, the owner crawled under the deck and used a flashlight to examine the opening. At the opening, she saw the presence of flies, and tore up boards on her front deck to access the crawl space. She found Patio's body four feet from the opening of the crawl space. Based upon her injuries, it appeared to the owner that a car might have hit Patio. (This search shows the benefit of training short-legged, small dog breeds who can crawl under decks and access areas that larger dogs are not able to reach.)

Tony
Cat found by "clearing" his territory

Tony, a ten-year-old outdoor-access cat, disappeared from his home in Aptos, California. Owner Catherine searched the area, but could not find Tony so she called me. I responded with search dog, Rachel, and conducted an extensive search of Tony's territory.

I had permission to search every yard within Tony's territory and determined that he was simply no longer in the area. This information helped me determine where to focus my search efforts. Once I knew that Tony was not trapped, injured, or deceased within his territory, I then turned to the most probable search area—a roofer's van that had been parked at Catherine's home with the doors open.

On the day that Tony vanished, a roofer had been working on Catherine's roof. He left his company van wide open, all day long, as he worked. Because Tony had previously climbed into vehicles with doors and windows left open, Catherine suspected that Tony might have climbed into the roofer's van.

Because Tony previously exhibited this behavior (of climbing into open cars) and because Rachel "cleared" Tony's territory and determined that he was no longer there, the high probability search area became the roofer's van. Catherine told me she had already called the roofer twice and asked him to look in his van for Tony, but he said Tony was not there. I told Catherine that if she wanted to get her cat back, she needed to be aggressive and risk being a pest. I told her to call the roofer back and ask him to tell her all of the locations where he had opened his van so that she could post flyers at those places.

Catherine went a step farther. She called the roofer and asked if she could come to his house to search the van herself. He said yes. When Catherine went over and looked in the van, she did not see Tony. But when she called him, she heard a "meow" response and Tony popped out from under a back seat in the van. He had been hiding in fear in the back of the van for three days!

This is a classic example of displaced cat behavior. Tony was displaced in an unfamiliar area (the back of a noisy van) and he had remained hidden and silent. Even when the roofer had opened his van and worked on two other roofs, Tony had not come out of his hiding place because he was terrified. This case is also an example of how a search dog can provide critical information (that the cat is no longer in the area) and how profiling the behavior of a specific cat (Tony was known to climb into open vehicles) can be used to help solve missing animal investigations.

Charley
Indoor-only cat found by cadaver alert

Charley, a cream-colored Himalayan indoor-only cat, escaped through an open door on November 12. I was contacted on November 14 and asked to respond, but I was out of town and not available until November 18, six days after Charley's escape.

Charley's profile was that she was panicked, hiding, and would most likely be found within a three-house radius of where she escaped. Charley's owner contacted an animal communicator who told her that Charley was alive and was hiding underneath a house four houses down. I instructed Charley's owner to set up humane traps in the immediate area and advised her that I'd respond the afternoon of November 18.

On the morning of November 18, Charley's owner talked to a second animal communicator who told her that a Hispanic woman in a brown house nearby was holding Charley. The communicator described the woman and the house. Charley's owner found a neighbor who fit the description, but the family denied having seen the cat.

I arrived on November 18 (along with one of our volunteers) and began to search with Rachel. We conducted an area search of the houses in the area with negative results. We then noticed an opening under the back fence that led into a wooded area. We began an area search of the wooded area and within 100 yards of the back fence and directly behind the house where she escaped, Rachel located fresh coyote scat. Approximately fifteen yards from the coyote scat, we spotted two cream-colored clumps of fur on the ground. Rachel alerted and pulled us up an embankment. Within ten feet of the clumps of fur found on the dirt road, Rachel located several clumps of white fur and a few internal organs.

By examining the remains that Rachel located, we determined the following information. First, the animal responsible for the kill site appeared to be a coyote. The presence of what appeared to be coyote feces, the nature of the tufts of fur at the kill site in close proximity to the cat's home, and the acknowledgment by neighbors that coyotes had been heard and seen in the area supported this hypothesis.

Second, the condition of the tissue and the presence of blow fly larvae on the tissues indicated that the prey had been killed at least forty-eight hours prior to our finding the remains. The fact that it had recently rained, yet the tissues were dried out was physical evidence that Charley was not alive that morning when the animal communicator claimed that Charley was still being held by a Hispanic woman in the neighborhood.

Finally, we sent the hair samples found at the kill site to a forensic hair examiner. The hair examiner positively identified the hair fibers as being cat hair. Unfortunately, we did not have an adequate sample of Charley's DNA to perform a DNA comparison test that would have given a positive identification and a conclusive answer to Charley's owner that the remains were definitely her cat.

Marmalade
Cat found by a MAR trailing Bloodhound

A diabetic cat, Marmalade, an indoor-only cat who escaped outdoors, was missing for a day when I was called and asked to respond. However, the terrain was too steep for me to work my dogs (due to an injury) and my primary volunteer pet detective, Becky Hiatt, was not immediately available.

The following day, two days after Marmalade escaped, Becky and I responded with my Bloodhound, A.J. I decided to use A.J. because he was a seasoned trailing dog who had found many missing people (read my first book, *The Lost Pet Chronicles* to learn more about A.J.'s trailing career).

Due to a disability, I had recently retired from police work. I knew that I would no longer be able to work A.J. on criminal or missing person cases and decided that, even though I had never used him on lost-pet cases, I had nothing to lose by seeing if he would follow a cat trail. I knew that of my three search dogs, A.J. was the best candidate for following a scent trail from point "A" to point "B." In this case, point "A" was the sliding glass door where Marmalade escaped and point "B" was where he was hiding. Although Rachel had proven herself in finding lost cats and Chase was beginning to solve lost-dog cases, A.J. was superior at following a scent trail. I was eager to give him a shot.

Becky had already worked Rachel on many cases, but had never handled A.J. She scented A.J. on Marmalade's bedding right outside of the sliding glass door as I observed and coached from a distance. *Within eight minutes*, A.J. found Marmalade. He dragged Becky (with Marmalade's owner behind her) through the back yard, down a ravine, crawled under a barbed wire fence, headed east into a grove of thick bushes, and found Marmalade's lifeless, concealed body.

As an aside, when I arrived on this case I immediately encountered an unsupportive family member. When I stepped out of my truck, the husband of Marmalade's owner didn't greet me with a "Hello" or a "How do you do," or even the words that pet detectives with trained search dogs often hear: "Wow, what a great idea!" Instead, he said flatly, "That dog will never find that cat." It was difficult to hear, especially when I had doubts myself as to whether A.J. would understand that I wanted him to trail a cat and not a human, but I knew we had to give it a shot. If you plan to train a dog for MAR work, be prepared to experience occasional resistance and skepticism from family, friends, and neighbors that you encounter while on a search.

Cali
Cat found near cadaver alert

Cali, a three-year-old black-and-white outdoor-access Calico cat, vanished from her home. Cali had an infection in her leg and was taking antibiotics. Her owner brought her into the house and attempted to contain her, but Cali escaped outside (her normal territory) the following day. Her owner had not been able to find her. By the time she discovered my services and I was able to respond, Cali had been missing for two weeks.

I was concerned because Cali's territory included roaming as far as two blocks from her home. In fact, Cali's owner would go for walks up to one mile from her house and Cali would follow. On a previous occasion, Cali had wandered over to a local elementary school three blocks away and was hanging around there.

This search took place before I had identified the silence factor —a pattern of behavior that I've since discovered is common with cats who are sick, injured, or panicked due to displacement. But thankfully, I did understand (from previous recoveries) that I still needed to make Cali's territory my target search area.

Conducting an area search, the volunteers and I searched Cali's yard with negative results. We moved to the house directly behind Cali's home and obtained permission from the neighbor to search in their backyard. While searching the screen-covered vents at the base of the home, cat detection dog Leo gave a decomposition alert. As I knelt down, I was able to detect the odor of decomposition. I also observed two flies at the base of the vents. Using a flashlight, we were able to see the carcass of something that was black-and-white underneath the house.

Cali's owner did not believe it was her cat. She could not understand how her cat could have been so close to home—within calling distance—and that Cali had not responded during the hours the owner had frantically called her. However, we learned that Cali routinely spent much time underneath this same house and that it was her outdoor litter box. We confirmed this by statements from the owner of the house (who had observed Cali in their yard) and by the amount of cat feces that we discovered when we crawled under the house and recovered Cali's body.

Cattiva
Cat found by cadaver alert, case solved by forensic anthropologist

Cattiva, a four-year-old chocolate Persian outdoor-access cat, disappeared from her home in Los Gatos, California. Cattiva and her family had recently moved to a wooded area of the Santa Cruz Mountains. Although coyotes were common in the general area, neighborhood cats ran freely and there had been no known cases of coyotes attacking cats in the immediate area.

Cattiva had disappeared on June 8 and on June 10 cat-detection dog, Leo, was dispatched to search Cattiva's territory. In the wooded area behind Cattiva's home and in an area where Cattiva's owners had already searched, Leo located a few brown tufts of fur, a classic sign of a coyote kill. Although they suspected the tufts belonged to Cattiva, her owners wanted more information. They hoped that they could find a carcass or more physical evidence than just a few tufts of brown fur. I was in New York at the time and was not able to respond.

On June 17, I responded with search dog, Rachel. We hoped that Rachel could provide further information by telling us whether there was the presence of blood, tissue, or bones in the area of the fur that Leo found. One of Rachel's natural decomposition alerts was to urinate when she detected human or animal decomposition. Upon entering the wooded area where Leo found the tufts of fur, Rachel located an area of interest, sniffed the ground, squatted and urinated. Upon closely examining the ground where Rachel sniffed, we located more tufts of fur and more evidence: a single animal bone. We photographed and collected the fur and the bone and prepared the evidence for further analysis.

In July I consulted with forensic anthropologist, Ann Galloway, Ph.D from the University of California, Santa Cruz Anthropology Department. Dr. Galloway examined the bone and determined that it was a femur bone from an adult cat. This was critical information for this investigation. The presence of chocolate colored tufts of fur along with a bone from an adult cat within Cattiva's territory was strong evidence that Cattiva had been killed by a predator. Because Cattiva shared her cabin with three other cats and we were not able to isolate anything with Cattiva's known DNA, we were not able to proceed with DNA testing to make a positive identification in this case.

Although forensic anthropologists are routinely used to analyze human remains in homicide investigations, the analysis of the feline bone in the Cattiva investigation was the first known case in which forensic anthropology was used to help a pet detective solve a missing animal investigation.

Gizmo
Cat found by cat detection dog

Gizmo, a two-year-old white, outdoor-access cat, vanished from his home in San Jose, California. Gizmo was blind in one eye and was an outdoor-access cat. However, Gizmo's territory was quite small and he was not known to venture very far. Gizmo had been missing for three days when I responded with an infrared camera, a listening device, and cat detection dog, Rachel.

Starting in Gizmo's yard, my volunteers and I began a systematic area search of Gizmo's territory. Upon entering the backyard three houses south of Gizmo's home, Rachel suddenly gave a strong alert that she had found a cat. Being a Weimaraner and "bird dog" bred to point at game, Rachel froze in a pointing stance. This was one of Rachel's natural methods of indicating that she was in the immediate scent pool of a cat.

Upon checking the brush area directly in front of Rachel, we found a fluffed up, frightened Gizmo who had apparently been hiding for three days inside an abandoned bathtub in the neighbor's backyard.

It is still unclear why Gizmo had not returned home. We speculated that he had been frightened out of his own yard and was too panicked to return home. Since this case, we've discovered many instances of cats who can be "displaced" into unfamiliar territory simply by being chased a few houses away. Depending on the temperament of the individual cat, some cats will hide and then return home once the coast is clear while other cats are so panicked by being displaced they are too afraid to come home. Sadly, many of these displaced, skittish cats are never found and are simply absorbed into the feral cat population.

Gizmo's family was ecstatic to have him safely home and they promptly turned him into an indoor-only cat! (The Gizmo rescue was recreated for the program *Miracle Pets* that aired on PAX TV and, later, on Animal Planet under the new title, *Animal Miracle*s.)

RESOURCES

MAR Evaluations and Certifications

Please note that these tests may change over time. Go to www.lostapet.org to view the current version of test that Missing Pet Partnership is using.

Missing Pet Partnership MAR K9 evaluation

1 = Very Poor   5 = Average/Sufficient   10 = Excellent

DOG:

DATE:

HANDLER/OWNER:

ADDRESS:

PHONE:

EMAIL:

EVALUATOR:

All testing is to be performed on-lead.

1.   STAY - Handler demonstrates good control (humane methods) of their dog. Handler places dog in sit or down stay (on long lead), leaves dog and walks 25 feet away while dog remains in place.
     1 2 3 4 5 6 7 8 9 10

Comments:

2. RECALL – Mild distraction is brought in while dog is in sit/down stay. Handler calls dog and dog ignores distraction and returns to the handler. Dog must demonstrate a reliable recall without handler pulling on lead.
   1 2 3 4 5 6 7 8 9 10

Comments:

3. FEAR – Dog is exposed to clanging noise (lid dropped on pan), sudden opening of umbrella, banging of spoon on pan, and/or banging of crutches or broom on ground. Dog must not show an excessive level of fear.
   PASS   FAIL

Comments:

4. HUMAN AGGRESSION – Stranger approaches dog and acts weird (or wears hat and overcoat or garbage bag with head poking out). Stranger approaches (but keeps safe distance) staring directly at dog with crutches or broom held overhead in the air in a threatening manner. Dog must not show excessive fear or aggression. Preferred response is friendly tail wagging, looking away, submission signals, etc.
   PASS   FAIL

Comments:

5. DOG AGGRESSION – Unfamiliar dog (on lead) approaches the dog. Dog in testing is friendly and does not show aggression (growling, barking, snapping, lunging, or raised hackles) toward the unfamiliar dog.
   PASS   FAIL

Comments:

6. DOG ATTRACTION – Target dog (on lead) who approaches the dog in testing is invited (through obvious body language) to PLAY with the dog. Dog's tail should be wagging, dipping, and he should show submissive signals and play language. Target dog is allowed to come up and play with the dog. When the target dog is suddenly jogged away, dog in testing should be focused and fixated on the target dog. Desired behaviors are signs of excitement like whining, jumping, and struggling to chase after the target dog.
1 2 3 4 5 6 7 8 9 10

Comments:

7. CAT INTEREST LEVEL – Dog is walked into the scent cone of a concealed, crated feline. Handler should be instructed to be silent and should not attempt to lead the dog (unless instructed) to the cat. Dog should show enough interest in the scent that he goes in to investigate on his own. Dog must show a physical reaction (butt wag, fixation, whining etc.) indicating strong interest and should remain focused on the crate. Dog should not show an aversion or fear of the cat.
1 2 3 4 5 6 7 8 9 10

Comments:

8. CAT AGGRESSION - This test should only be performed with dogs who are known to be friendly with and/or live with cats. Strange cat in harness/on lead is walked near dog. Dog shows excitement and friendly interest (but not aggression) toward the cat. Dog is allowed to sniff/approach cat from behind but does not snap, lunge, or attempt to hurt the cat. Dog (on long lead) should be totally fixated on the cat.

PASS   FAIL

Comments:

SUMMARY OF EVALUATION

COMMENTS ON EVALUTAION:

EVALUATOR RECOMMENDATIONS: (CHECK ONE)

[ ]   CAT DETECTION DOG

[ ]   TRAILING DOG

[ ]   DUAL PURPOSE DOG

[ ]   MAGNET DOG

[ ]   TARGET DOG

[ ]   FAILED EVALUATION

Missing Pet Partnership cat detection dog certification test

1. FEAR – Dogs is exposed to clanging noise (lid dropped on pan), sudden opening of umbrella, banging of spoon on pan, and/or banging of crutches or broom on ground. Dog must not show an excessive level of fear.

Date Demonstrated:

Comments:

2. HUMAN AGGRESSION – Stranger approaches dog and acts weird (or wears hat and overcoat or garbage bag with head poking out). Stranger approaches (but keeps safe distance) staring directly at dog with crutches or broom held overhead in the air in a threatening manner. Dog must not show excessive fear or aggression. Preferred response is friendly tail wagging, looking away, submission signals, etc.

Date Demonstrated:

Comments:

3. DOG AGGRESSION – Strange dog (on lead) approaches the dog. Dog in testing does not show aggression (growling, barking, snapping, lunging, or raised hackles) toward the strange dog.

Date Demonstrated:

Comments:

4. CAT INTEREST LEVEL – Dog is walked into the scent cone of a concealed, crated feline. Handler should be instructed to be silent and should not attempt to lead the dog (unless instructed) to the cat. Dog should show intense interest in the scent of the cat. Dog must show a physical reaction (butt wag, fixation, whining etc.) and should remain focused on the crate. Dog should not show an aversion or fear of the cat.

Date Demonstrated:

Comments:

5. CAT AGGRESSION - This test should only be performed with dogs who are known to be friendly with or co-habitat with cats. Strange cat in harness/on lead is walked near dog. Dog shows interest in (but not aggression toward) the cat. Dog is allowed to approach/sniff/lick cat but does not snap, lunge, or attempt to hurt or chase the cat. Dog should be fixated on the cat but under the handler's control.

Date Demonstrated:

Comments:

6. DECOMPOSITION SCENT – Jar with cat decomposition scent is concealed in bushes and dog walked past the jar. Dog must alert on the scent, find it, and give a physical indication (signal) by pawing, pushing, or dig-digging at the jar.

Date Demonstrated:

Comments:

7. LIVE CAT SEARCH TEST – Cat is crated and concealed within a specific five-acre search area. Location will contain many areas of concealment and cover with human and animal distractions.

Search dog will be given one-hour to locate the crated cat, demonstrating the following:

(a) CHECK THIS – Handler must be able to direct the dog to "check this" in which case the dog will investigate/sniff the location where handler points.

Date Demonstrated:

(b) READABLE ALERT – Handler is able to read their dog when he detects the air scent of a cat.

Date Demonstrated:

(c) INDICATION – Dog gives a consistent behavior (sit, down, tail wiggles, whine, etc.) when he locates a cat. Handler can describe this indication prior to testing and dog performs this behavior upon finding a cat.

Date Demonstrated:

(d) HANDLER STRATEGY – Handler properly directs their dog to check potential hiding places when searching areas of concealment for the hidden cat.

Date Demonstrated:

(e) LOCATES CAT – Search dog locates the crated cat within the allotted time.

Date Demonstrated:

EVALUATOR ASSESSMENT:

[ ]   CERTIFIED MAR CAT DETECTION DOG

Date:

Evaluator:

[ ]   NOT RECOMMENDED FOR SEARCH WORK

Date:

Evaluator:

Missing Pet Partnership MAR trailing dog certification test

1. FEAR – Dogs is exposed to clanging noise (lid dropped on pan), sudden opening of umbrella, banging of spoon on pan, and/or banging of crutches or broom on ground. Dog must not show an excessive level of fear.

Date Demonstrated:

Comments:

2. HUMAN AGGRESSION – Stranger approaches dog and acts weird (or wears hat and overcoat or garbage bag with head poking out). Stranger approaches (but keeps safe distance) staring directly at dog with crutches or broom held overhead in the air in a threatening manner. Dog must not show excessive fear or aggression. Preferred response is friendly tail wagging, looking away, submission signals, etc.

Date Demonstrated:

Comments:

3. DOG AGGRESSION – Strange dog (on lead) approaches the dog. Search dog does not show aggression (growling, barking, snapping, lunging, or raised hackles) toward the strange dog.

Date Demonstrated:

Comments:

4. DOG ATTRACTION – Target dog (on lead) is allowed to come up and play with the search dog. When the target dog is suddenly jogged away, search dog should be focused and fixated on the target dog. Desired behaviors are signs of excitement like whining, jumping and struggling to chase after the target dog.

Date Demonstrated:

Comments:

5. DECOMPOSITION SCENT – Jar with cat or dog decomposition scent is hidden in bushes and search dog led past it. Dog must alert, find the jar, and give a physical indication (signal) by pawing, pushing, or dig-digging at the jar.

Date Demonstrated:

Comments:

6. TRAILING TEST – Without the handler knowing where the trail is, search dog must work an urban scent trail, a portion of which is laid in a residential area. Trail must be at least 24-hours old, at least ¾ miles in length, and have at least three intersections and at least three turns in direction. Search dog will be given 90 minutes to locate the target dog. Handler and dog must demonstrate the following:

(a) READABLE BODY LANGUAGE – Handler is able to read their dog when he is on the correct scent trail and when he loses the scent trail. Prior to test, handler is able to articulate their dog's body language when he is on the scent vs. when he is off the scent.

Date Demonstrated:

Comments:

(b) NEGATIVE INDICATION – Handler is able to read their dog when she is on the correct scent trail and when she loses the scent trail. Prior to test, handler is able to articulate what their dog does to indicate that she has lost the scent.

Date Demonstrated:

Comments:

(c) LOCATES TARGET DOG – Search dog locates the target dog within the allotted time.

Date Demonstrated:

Comments:

EVALUATOR ASSESSMENT:

[ ]   CERTIFIED MAR TRAILING DOG

Date:

Evaluator:

[ ]   NOT RECOMMENDED FOR SEARCH WORK

Date:

Evaluator:

Suggested Reading

If you're serious about training a search dog, you should learn everything you can about the topic. Keep in mind, however, that trying to articulate in writing how to train a dog to detect or trail a scent is not an easy task. Here's a list of additional books I suggest that you read. Most of these books can be ordered through Dogwise at www.dogwise.com.

Scent and the Scenting Dog by William Syrotuck. This is an old classic known as the "scent bible" for search dog handlers. While the author's concepts of trailing dogs are a bit off target, the air scenting and olfactory information is outstanding.

Scenting on the Wind: Scentwork for Hunting Dogs by Susan Bulanda. This is a good book that contains information about how scent is dispersed.

Ready to Serve, Ready to Save! Strategies of Real-Life Search & Rescue Missions by Susan Bulanda. This is an interesting book that dissects actual search-and-rescue cases and contains search strategies, including what went right and what went wrong.

A Practical Guide to Training and Working the Trailing Dog by John Lutenberg and Linda Porter. This is probably the best book out there on how to train a dog in scent discrimination trailing work for finding people. If you plan to train a MAR trailing dog then you need to read this book!

Common Scents: Bloodhounds in Law Enforcement by Jerry Nichols & Milica Wilson is a spiral bound training guide designed for training police Bloodhounds. It has great information about training Bloodhounds to trail but it's self published and only available for purchase on-line through the Law Enforcement Bloodhound Association (LEBA) at www.leba98.com.

Sherlock Bones by John Keane. This book is now out of print (1979) but you can find copies on-line through used book stores. It contains great stories from one of the first pet detectives who in the 1970's conducted shelter checks, stakeouts, and some risky and unorthodox techniques to recover lost pets.

The Power of Positive Dog Training by Pat Miller. This is an excellent, easy to read book that explains how and why positive dog training (including clicker training) works. Includes tips and exercises that will help you develop a working relationship with your dog through positive methods instead of fear and punishment.

The Lost Pet Chronicles: Adventures of a K-9 Cop Turned Pet Detective by Kat Albrecht with Jana Murphy. This is my memoirs. It's a great read and I'd be a lousy author if I didn't suggest that you read it! If you enjoyed reading the lost dog and cat case studies (in Chapter 14) then you'll enjoy this book.

Suggested Equipment
The following is a list of equipment that you'll need in order to train and work your MAR search dog. The items will vary depending on what discipline you plan to train.

RELFECTIVE SEARCH COLLAR: For dual purpose dogs you'll need to create a special search collar with a very small cat bell (used on cat collars to scare off birds) that will help cue him that he'll be conducting an area search. I suggest an orange web collar with a highly visible, florescent orange reflective strip sewn into the collar. Use the smallest, quietest bell possible – one that makes enough noise that your dog will hear it but not one that will let neighborhood dogs know that a dog is approaching. The purpose of this bell is so your dog can distinguish the difference between conducting an area search and a trailing assignment. This will be a collar that you only put on your dog right before you begin working him on cat detection cases.

HARNESS: You will need a tracking harness for your dog. You can find a variety of tracking dog harnesses available on-line by using a search engine and typing in "dog + tracking harness." Leather is always nice but nylon requires less care and is less expensive.

SHABRACK VEST/PATCHES: A shabrack (I've also heard it called a "shadrack") is a small vest used to identify your dog a working search dog. The color that you select for a shabrack should be orange. Because MAR search dogs are NOT search-and-rescue dogs, you should avoid patches that say "search-and-rescue," "Police K9," or "Rescue." The only patch that you should utilize for a MAR search dog would be a patch or reflective strip that states either "SEARCH" or "SEARCH DOG." You can find vests and patches like this through Search Gear at www.search-gear.com. Under "Dog Products" you'll find the dog vests (normal style, bikini vest, or mesh style all acceptable). Constructed of two layers of bright orange Cordura nylon. Sizes are Small up to 30lbs, Small/Medium 30-50lbs, Medium 50-75lbs, Large 76-125lbs.

HARNESS/VEST COMBINATION: For larger dogs, you might opt to purchase a tracking harness that has the words SEARCH included on the harness. Known as the "Patrol K9" harness (available through Canine Outfitters at www.canineoutfitters.com) this harness relieves you from purchasing both a harness and a vest; however, because they were designed for police dogs, they are only available for medium and large size dogs. You should select two Velcro, reflective strips that have the word SEARCH printed on them.

LONG LINE: You will want to have at least one 30-foot long lead. Again, leather is nice but nylon webbing works just as well. You can select a thin web line or you can even utilize a thick web "lunge line" – a nylon lead with a heavy snap that is sold at saddle shops and used for training horses in a process known as lunging. I use a thin nylon web line for my cat detection and dual purpose dogs because they work well when working through bushes and in backyards. For my trailing dogs when working urban searches, I prefer to use a horse lunge line because it is heavier and helps me manage working a larger dog around cars and traffic.

STERILE GAUZE PADS: You will need to stock up on boxes of 3 X 3 sterile gauze pads. Presenting a clean scent to your dual purpose and trailing dog is critical so sterile gauze pads are a must for training and for actual search operations.

LAYTEX GLOVES: Found wherever medical supplies are available, you (and your target dog handlers) will need to use disposable gloves (latex or similar type) to prevent your scent from being directly transferred to the scent article that you prepare for your dog in training and on actual searches.

LEATHER GLOVES: These are optional, but I strongly suggest that you wear some type of leather glove when handling a dog – especially if you use a lead made of nylon webbing. Should the lead somehow get yanked through your hands, having gloves will protect your hands from rope burns. I use leather "Franklin" brand baseball batting gloves because they have a snug fit and are very light weight. In addition, for animal decomposition scent training, you will probably want to keep a pair of yard gloves (cloth or leather) to use for handling decomposition material only.

CLICKER: For animal decomposition training you will want to purchase a few clickers. These small plastic rectangular devices make a loud double "click" sound and are available through most pet stores or on-line through various sites related to "clicker training."

TREAT POUCH: You will need a method to carry dog treats so that you can easily access treats for your dog. I use a radio chest harness with a zippered pouch (made by Lone Peak Designs www.lonepeakpacks.com) because in addition to holding my baggie of treats it also holds my keys, cell phone, and a small radio. Another option is to wear a fanny pack or to purchase a treat pouch with a clip for your belt.

LOST PET RESCUE VEST: This is a vest that YOU will wear to clearly mark you so people will realize you are training or working a search dog. A highly florescent orange vest with LOST PET RESCUE (that you'll have silk screened) on the back is a must have when working near traffic. I like the "Supplex Multi-Pocket Command Vest" available at www. searchgear.com or the "Ten pocket tactical vest with reflective striping" available at www.animal-care.com.

Clicker Training

Here's where you can find clicker training resources including books, videos, trainers, and clicker training seminars:
Karen Pryor – www.clickertraining.com
Pat Miller – Peaceable Paws – www.peaceablepaws.com
Gary Wilkes – www.clickandtreat.com
Angelica Steinker – www.courteouscanine.com
The Association of Pet Dog Trainers (APDT) – www.apdt.com

Suggested MAR Dog Trainers

Here's a list of professional, successful MAR dog handlers that I recommend for MAR dog training work and for evaluation/certification of MAR dogs. They are each highly skilled at training dogs to locate lost pets.

Kat Albrecht (Fresno, California or Seattle, Washington) – info@katal-brecht.com. It is probable that I will be relocating to Seattle, WA some-time in 2008 and that my availability for private training sessions will be limited. Feel free to e-mail me at info@katalbrecht.com to check my status.

Landa Coldiron—(Los Angeles, California)—Lost Pet Detection – (818) 442-2952—www.lostpetdetection.com—email caninesearchdog@hot-mail.com. Landa is an experienced MAR Technician who has trained MAR trailing dogs, cat detection dogs, and dual purpose dogs. She's worked many successful cases—finding both lost cats and dogs. When she is not out using her dogs to track lost pets Landa is evaluating and training more MAR dogs and students.

Tara Walldorff—(Hastings, Michigan)—Forked River Missing Animal Response—(269) 948-4054 or visit their web page by going to www.lostadog.com and clicking on Barry County. Tara is an experienced SAR dog handler, tracking student (man and animal tracks), and MAR Tech-nician who has worked successful cases with her dogs. She trains with a group of experienced SAR dog handlers and is occasionally available for MAR dog training.

Laura Totis—(Baltimore, Maryland)—LJT Training—www.ljttraining.com—(410) 239-4746—email vtotis@carr.org. Laura is a certified MAR Technician and experienced search-and-rescue dog handler/trainer. Since 2004, Laura has successfully used her search dogs to track lost pets (prior to that she worked her search-and-rescue dogs for years in finding lost people). Laura actively trains dogs in MAR work, holding seminars and conducting one-on-one lessons.

Becky Hiatt—(Santa Cruz, California)—(831) 336-3243. Becky is a certified MAR Technician with over four years experience in handling and training MAR search dogs and was my primary assistant and dog handler when I worked the searches featured in the book *The Lost Pet Chronicles*.

Cathy Orde—(Centennial, Wyoming)—(307) 761-1799—e-mail or-diewy@aol.com. Cathy is a certified MAR Technician with six years of SAR trailing dog experience and drug detection dog training. Cathy has worked successful cases finding both missing people and lost pets and is available for one-on-one MAR dog training and testing.

Vicki Wooters—(Malvern, Pennsylvania)—(484) 343-5204—e-mail wooters2@comcast.net. Vicki is a professional dog trainer and SAR dog handler with two years experience in training and handling MAR dogs. Vicki has worked successful lost person and lost pet cases with her search dogs and is available for one-on-one MAR dog training.Author Biography

Acknowledgments
Most nonfiction books consist of the work of many people, not just the work of the author. This book, which I started back in 1998, is no different. I would like to thank the following people for their contributions to this book:

To all my SAR dog instructors, National Police Bloodhound Association instructors, and my three search dogs, Rachel, A.J., and Chase, for teaching me everything I needed to know about scent and search dogs. To Jeanne Mason, Stacey Dorsey, Jeff Schettler, and Judy Schettler, thanks for helping me make the difficult decision to transition from SAR to MAR. Jeff thanks also for graciously providing the statistics on your trailing work with Ronin—God rest his soul!

To Becky Hiatt, thank you for your friendship, for handling my search dogs when I wasn't able to, and for ultimately helping me recruit, evaluate, and train the first batch of search dogs from Half Moon Bay.

To the 1999-2000 Half Moon Bay pet detectives—Sheryl Carver and Leo, Jo Danehy and Kelsey, Danielle Diebert and Gyp, and Judy Butler and Phantom—thank you for letting me experiment with training concepts. I learned so much from both you and your dogs!

To the 2000-2001 Simi Valley pet detectives—Elena Cox, Electra Werthman, Dave Dowding, Pamela Collins, Terry Long, Linda Seiler, Shirley Andrew, Andrea Andrew, Faith Arnold, Susan Knoll, Claudine Singer, Joe Dantona, and Laura Bourhenne—thank you for believing in the concept of MAR and for the time you invested in training your dogs. I'm so sorry that my job was terminated and that I wasn't able to stay and help finish the training of you and your dogs.

To the 2001-2007 Missing Pet Partnership Fresno pet detectives—Stephen Schwartz, Hardin Weaver, Cannon and Madeline Hill, Terri Williams, Shirley Kirk, Lindy Kirk, Tammi Creamier, Joyce Bicknell, Nancy

Weber, Claudine Randazzo, Antoinette Taillac, Kelly Brannigan, Susan Tiftick, Barbara, Thacker, Joanne Thacker, Dennis Cook, Jim Merson, Beverlee Bargamian, Jill Buchanan, Betsy Brandt-Kreutz, and Kathy Pinto—thanks for the many hours you've all invested in walking target dogs, hiding and watching target cats, running behind trailing dogs, working cat detection dogs, and volunteering to help with various MPP projects. Thanks for listening to me whine when things just didn't seem to be going my way! Your support, especially in the midst of my worst struggles, helped to sustain me.

To all the national and international Missing Pet Partnership (and Pet Hunters International) MAR Technicians who trained their dogs by using simple rough drafts of just a few chapters from this book to train their dogs—thanks for your patience. I wish you nothing but happy scent trails as you move forward in your new pet detective endeavors!

To my sister Susan Gibson, thank you for donating your artistic talent by creating all of the illustrations in this book. May God richly bless your artistic talent and open the doors for your ministry! To my oldest sister Diane Albrecht Huckleberry, thank you for your copyedit work and for managing my business affairs.

I owe a big thank you to Hardin Weaver and Jill Buchanan who provided the vast majority of photographs used in this book. Thanks also to Daisy Villicana, Jan Jarvis, Cannon Hill, Susan Tiftick, Melinda Hearne, Dani Deibert, Don Harris from UCSC Photography, Shmuel Thaler from the Santa Cruz Sentinel, Vicky Vaughn, Janice Smith, and Jane Sokolow for the photographs that they provided. Thanks to those who donated several hours posing for the training sequence photos—Susan Tiftick with Lucy, Jackie Villicana with Yipper, Daisy Villicana with Annie and Lilly, Hardin Weaver with Susie, Cathy Orde with Zoe, Landa Coldiron with Ellie Mae and Apache, Charlot McClendon with Banjo, Teresa Bressoud with Coon, Becky Hiatt with Rachel and Chase, Betsy Brandt-Kruetz with "Q", Jill Buchanan with Dixie, Michelle Hess, Katie Kostik, and Stephen Schwartz with Cinder.

Thanks also to my literary agent Jeffery Kleinman from Folio Literary Management for your guidance in the early stages of this book, to publisher Charlene Woodward for believing in this book, to Larry Woodward for the great editing job that you've done, and to Nate Woodward for coordinating the layout design. Thanks also to Ginny Guidry for putting the final polish on the manuscript with your copyedit work.

The majority of work on this book was completed during an incredibly difficult time of my life. I want to thank my Pastors Randy Freeman and Lynn Freeman of NewSong Christian Center and my TLC friends—Linda Raymundo, Kathy Barayuga, Evelyn Chandler, and Zebora Tingle—for their prayers and support. And last of all, I would like to give all glory and honor to Jesus Christ—who taught me everything I needed to know about having a passion for finding the lost!

Author Biography

Kathy "Kat" Albrecht is a former police Bloodhound handler, search-and-rescue manager, and police officer-turned-pet detective. Since 1989 she and her search dogs have successfully located criminals, physical evidence, missing persons, and missing pets for both police agencies and private clients. In 1995, Albrecht and A.J., her Bloodhound, received the National Police Bloodhound Association's Lifesaving Award after A.J. tracked down and saved the life of a man who attempted suicide. Then after an experience in 1996 where A.J. escaped and was lost, Albrecht pioneered the application of innovative, law enforcement-based techniques to solve missing pet investigations like cat detection dogs, scent tracking dogs, amplified listening-devices, search cameras, behavioral profiling, search probability theory, and forensic applications like DNA testing and the use of forensic anthropologists. In 2001, Albrecht founded Missing Pet Partnership, a national nonprofit organization that is working to develop community-based lost pet services while also managing the first-ever pet detective academy. Her inspirational work has been featured on Animal Planet shows like Animal Miracles, K9 to Five, and Breed All About It and in magazines like PARADE, National Examiner, Ladies' Home Journal, Reader's Digest, and BARK. Albrecht resides in Clovis, California with her three dogs and three cats.

BEHAVIOR & TRAINING

ABC's of Behavior Shaping; Fundamentals of Training; Proactive Behavior Mgmt, DVD. Ted Turner

Aggression In Dogs: Practical Mgmt, Prevention & Behaviour Modification. Brenda Aloff

Am I Safe? DVD. Sarah Kalnajs

Behavior Problems in Dogs, 3rd ed. William Campbell

Brenda Aloff's Fundamentals: Foundation Training for Every Dog, DVD. Brenda Aloff

Bringing Light to Shadow. A Dog Trainer's Diary. Pam Dennison

Canine Body Language. A Photographic Guide to the Native Language of Dogs. Brenda Aloff

Clicked Retriever. Lana Mitchell

Dog Behavior Problems: The Counselor's Handbook. William Campbell

Dog Friendly Gardens, Garden Friendly Dogs. Cheryl Smith

Dog Language, An Encyclopedia of Canine Behavior. Roger Abrantes

Evolution of Canine Social Behavior, 2nd ed. Roger Abrantes

Give Them a Scalpel and They Will Dissect a Kiss, DVD. Ian Dunbar

Guide To Professional Dog Walking And Home Boarding. Dianne Eibner

Language of Dogs, DVD. Sarah Kalnajs

Mastering Variable Surface Tracking, Component Tracking (2 bk set). Ed Presnall

Mindful Dog Teaching: Reflections on the Relationships we Share with our Dogs. Claudeen McAuliffe

My Dog Pulls. What Do I Do? Turid Rugaas

New Knowledge of Dog Behavior (reprint). Clarence Pfaffenberger

On Talking Terms with Dogs: Calming Signals, 2nd edition. Turid Rugaas

On Talking Terms with Dogs: What Your Dog Tells You, DVD. Turid Rugaas

Positive Perspectives: Love Your Dog, Train Your Dog. Pat Miller

Positive Training for Show Dogs: Building a Relationship for Success. Vicki Ronchette

Predation and Family Dogs, DVD. Jean Donaldson

Really Reliable Recall. Train Your Dog to Come When Called, DVD. Leslie Nelson

Right on Target. Taking Dog Training to a New Level. Mandy Book & Cheryl Smith

Stress in Dogs. Martina Scholz & Clarissa von Reinhardt

The Dog Trainer's Resource: The APDT Chronicle of the Dog Collection. Mychelle Blake (*ed*)

Therapy Dogs: Training Your Dog To Reach Others.
Kathy Diamond Davis
Training Dogs, A Manual (reprint). Konrad Most
Training the Disaster Search Dog. Shirley Hammond
Try Tracking: The Puppy Tracking Primer. Carolyn Krause
Visiting the Dog Park, Having Fun, and Staying Safe. Cheryl S. Smith
When Pigs Fly. Train Your Impossible Dog. Jane Killion
Winning Team. A Guidebook for Junior Showmanship. Gail Haynes
Working Dogs (reprint). Elliot Humphrey & Lucien Warner

HEALTH & ANATOMY, SHOWING
An Eye for a Dog. Illustrated Guide to Judging Purebred Dogs. Robert Cole
Annie On Dogs! Ann Rogers Clark
Canine Cineradiography DVD. Rachel Page Elliott
Canine Massage: A Complete Reference Manual.
Jean-Pierre Hourdebaigt
Canine Terminology (reprint). Harold Spira
Dog In Action (reprint). Macdowell Lyon
Dogsteps DVD. Rachel Page Elliott
Performance Dog Nutrition: Optimize Performance With Nutrition.
Jocelynn Jacobs
Puppy Intensive Care: A Breeder's Guide To Care Of Newborn Puppies. Myra
Savant Harris
Raw Dog Food: Make It Easy for You and Your Dog. Carina MacDonald
Raw Meaty Bones. Tom Lonsdale
Shock to the System. The Facts About Animal Vaccination...
Catherine O'Driscoll
The History and Management of the Mastiff. Elizabeth Baxter & Pat Hoffman
Work Wonders. Feed Your Dog Raw Meaty Bones. Tom Lonsdale
Whelping Healthy Puppies, DVD. Sylvia Smart

Dogwise.com is your complete source for dog books on the web!

2,000+ titles, fast shipping, and excellent customer service.

Welcome | Featured Titles | Shows & Info | Publishing | Bargain Books | Help/Contact

Phone in your Order! 1.800.776.2665 8am-4pm PST / 11am-7pm EST

Be the First to Hear the News!
Have New Product and Promotion
Announcements Emailed to You.
Click Here To Sign Up!

Free Shipping for Orders over $75 - click here for more information!

Win a $25 Dogwise credit - click here to find out how!

Search Dogwise

Everything ▼

Browse Dogwise

Books & Products
* By Subject
* Dogwise Picks
* Best Sellers
* Best New Titles
Book Reviews
* Find Out How
Resources & Info
* Dogwise Forums
* Dogwise Newsletters
* Dogwise Email List
* Customer Reading Lists
* Dog Show Schedule
* Let Us Know About Your Book or DVD
* Become an Affiliate
* APDT, CPDT
* IAABC
* CAPPDT
Help & Contacts
* About Us
* Contact Us
* Shipping Policy

Employee Picks!
See which books the Dogwise staff members love to read.
* Click Here!

Dog Show Supplies from The 3C's
* Visit the 3c's Website
* View our selection of 3c products.

Save up to 80% on Bargain Books! Click here for Sale, Clearance and hard to find Out of Print titles!
* Click Here!

Prefer to order by phone? Call Us!
1-800-776-2665
8AM - 4PM M-F Pacific Time

Featured New Titles

STRESS IN DOGS - LEARN HOW DOGS SHOW STRESS AND WHAT YOU CAN DO TO HELP, by Martina Scholz & Clarissa von Reinhardt
Item: DTB909
Is stress causing your dog's behavior problems? Research shows that as with humans, many behavioral problems in dogs are stress-related. Learn how to recognize when your dog is stressed, what factors cause stress in dogs, and strategies you can utilize in training and in your daily life with your dog to reduce stress.
Price: $14.95 more information...

SUCCESS IS IN THE PROOFING - A GUIDE FOR CREATIVE AND EFFECTIVE TRAINING, by Debby Quigley & Judy Ramsey
Item: DTO230
The success is indeed in the proofing! Proofing is an essential part of training, but one that is often overlooked or not worked on enough. We all know the story of the dog who can perform a variety of behaviors perfectly in the backyard but falls apart in the obedience ring. This book is full of great ideas and strategies to help your dog do his best no matter what the distractions or conditions may be. Whether competing in Rally or Obedience, trainers everywhere will find this very portable and user friendly book an indispensable addition to their tool box.
Price: $19.95 more information...

REALLY RELIABLE RECALL DVD, by Leslie Nelson
Item: DTB810P
From well-known trainer Leslie Nelson! Easy to follow steps to train your dog to come when it really counts, in an emergency. Extra chapters for difficult to train breeds and training class instructors.
Price: $29.95 more information...

THE DOG TRAINERS RESOURCE - APDT CHRONICLE OF THE DOG COLLECTION, by Mychelle Blake, Editor
Item: DTB880
The modern professional dog trainer needs to develop expertise in a wide variety of fields: learning theory, training techniques, classroom strategies, marketing, community relations, and business development and management. This collection of articles from APDT's Chronicle of the Dog will prove a valuable resource for trainers and would-be trainers.
Price: $24.95 more information...

SHAPING SUCCESS - THE EDUCATION OF AN UNLIKELY CHAMPION, by Susan Garrett
Item: DTA260
Written by one of the world's best dog trainers, Shaping Success gives an excellent explanation of the theory behind animal learning as Susan Garrett trains a high-energy Border Collie puppy to be an agility champion. Buzzy's story both entertains and demonstrates how to apply some of the most up-to-date dog training methods in the real world. Clicker training!
Price: $24.95 more information...

FOR THE LOVE OF A DOG - UNDERSTANDING EMOTION IN YOU AND YOUR BEST FRIEND, by Patricia McConnell
Item: DTB890
Sure to be another bestseller. Trish McConnell's latest book takes a look at canine emotions and body language. Like all her books, this one is written in a way that the average dog owner can follow but brings the latest scientific information that trainers and dog enthusiasts can use.
Price: $24.95 more information...

HELP FOR YOUR FEARFUL DOG: A STEP-BY-STEP GUIDE TO HELPING YOUR DOG CONQUER HIS FEARS, by Nicole Wilde
Item: DTB878
From popular author and trainer Nicole Wilde. A comprehensive guide to the treatment of canine anxiety, fears, and phobias. Chock full of photographs and illustrations and written in a down-to-earth, humorous style.
Price: $24.95 more information...

FAMILY FRIENDLY DOG TRAINING - A SIX WEEK PROGRAM FOR YOU AND YOUR DOG, by Patricia McConnell & Aimee Moore
Item: DTB917
A six-week program to get people and dogs off on the right paw! Includes trouble-shooting tips for what to do when your dog doesn't respond as expected. This is a book that many trainers will want their students to read.
Price: $11.95 more information...

THE LANGUAGE OF DOGS - UNDERSTANDING CANINE BODY LANGUAGE AND OTHER COMMUNICATION SIGNALS DVD SET, by Sarah Kalnajs
Item: DTB875P
Features a presentation and extensive footage of a variety of breeds showing hundreds of examples of canine behavior and body language. Perfect for dog owners or anyone who handles dogs or encounters them regularly while on the job.
Price: $39.95 more information...

Made in the USA
Middletown, DE
09 August 2024

58826089R00139